MOTORSPORTS ENCYCLOPEDIAS

THE MONSTER TRUCKS ENCYCLOPEDIA

BY ASHLEY KUEHL

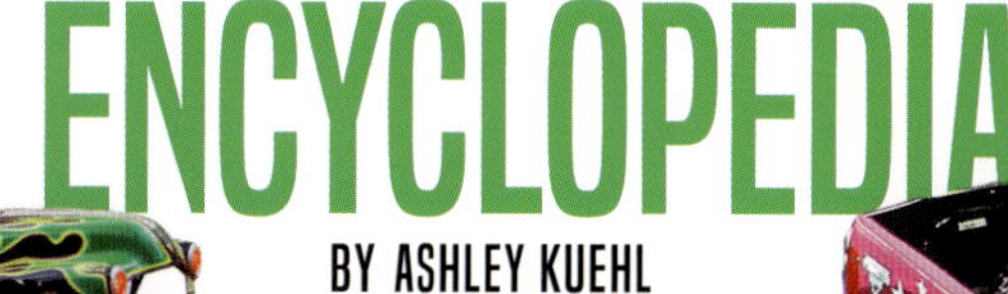

Encyclopedias

An Imprint of Abdo Reference
abdobooks.com

TABLE OF CONTENTS

BLUE THUNDER
MONSTER JAM
MONSTERJAM.COM
BKT

HISTORY OF MONSTER TRUCKS

In the 1970s, a Missouri man named Bob Chandler loved driving in places with no roads. Sometimes, his pickup truck would need repairs. But it wasn't always easy to find parts. So, in 1975, Bob and his wife Marilyn opened a shop. Four-wheel truck drivers could get parts and service. When parts on Bob's truck broke, he fixed or replaced them with new or different parts. Each repair made his truck bigger and stronger. Before he knew it, Bob had built Bigfoot, a truck with 4-foot (1-m) tires!

Bob wanted to try driving Bigfoot over cars. He and a friend made a video of the crunch. In 1981, an event promoter saw the video. He asked Bob to smash cars at a tractor pulling event. Around this time, an event announcer called Bigfoot a "monster truck." The name stuck.

Bigfoot crushing cars

A 1952 Ford truck was used to build Grave Digger.

Another historic truck was born in 1982. Dennis Anderson had a rusty 1952 Ford pickup truck. Anderson worked on a farm, and he started adding old, unused tractor parts to his truck. Soon he had built Grave Digger. Anderson became known for wild racing and being willing to put his truck through nearly anything. He started to earn money from competing and winning races.

Over the next few years, more people built monster trucks. Bigger races were organized. The sport was growing.

MONSTER TRUCK TRIVIA

Mud bogging is racing through the mud. It is popular in some places in the United States.

In 1987, Bob Chandler and other drivers wanted to make some safety standards for everyone. They created a group of 49 drivers and owners called the Monster Truck Racing Association (MTRA). MTRA put together a safety and rule book. Monster truck racing was becoming a respected sport.

Monster truck racing grew. In 1988, TNT Motorsports set up the first official monster truck competition, the Monster Truck Challenge. ESPN broadcast the races on television. This was

Frankenstein monster truck crushes cars in 1985.

A monster truck at a rally in 1989.

the first time trucks were racing for points. In 1991, the United States Hot Rod Association (USHRA) bought TNT Motorsports. It continued to show monster truck events on television.

In 1995, the USHRA started a series called Monster Jam. Then, in 2000, the group hosted the first ever Monster Jam World Finals in Las Vegas. At the World Finals, monster trucks compete in races and stunt contests to find out which one is the best.

In 2008, the corporation Feld Entertainment bought Monster Jam. This created change in the industry. Many trucks and teams joined up with Monster Jam. Others stayed independent. These days, Monster Jam is the biggest tour in monster trucks.

TIMELINE

1982

Dennis Anderson started building Grave Digger from a rusted old 1952 Ford pickup.

1975

Bob Chandler built Bigfoot out of his Ford F-250.

1987

People started racing their monster trucks, instead of just using them to smash cars.

1970s   **1980s**   **1990s**

1981

Bob Chandler drove Bigfoot over two junk cars in Missouri for the first time. An announcer called Bigfoot a "monster truck," the first use of this term.

1988

The Monster Truck Challenge became the first official monster truck racing event. ESPN showed it on television.

2008
Feld Entertainment bought Monster Jam. Feld already owned Ringling Bros. and Disney on Ice.

2012
Bigfoot 20 became the first electric monster truck.

2000s

2010s

2020s

1995
Monster Jam started touring as a monster truck show.

DIAGRAM OF A MONSTER TRUCK

Monster trucks have some of the same parts as any other truck. Other parts are unique to monster trucks.

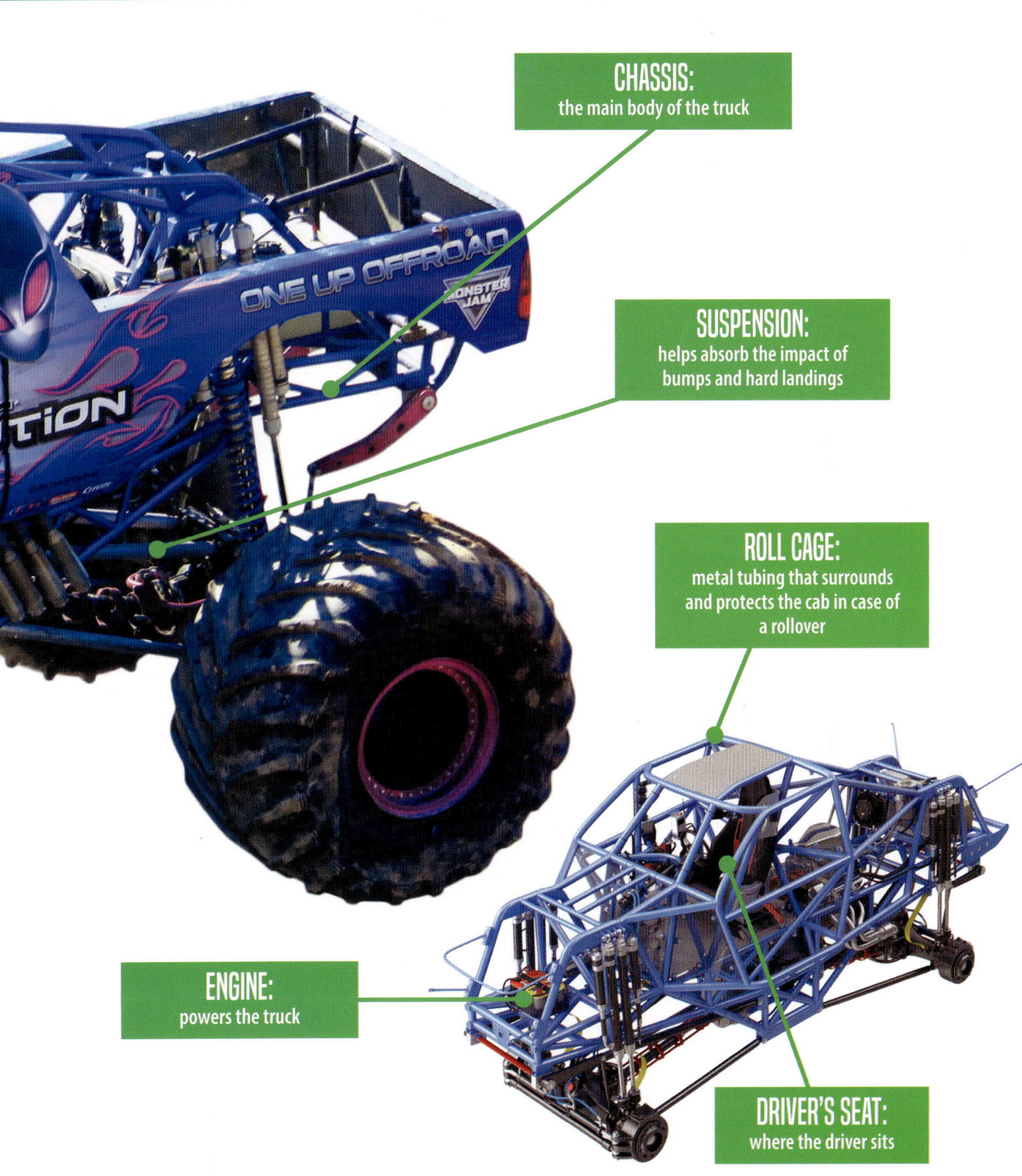

CHASSIS: the main body of the truck

SUSPENSION: helps absorb the impact of bumps and hard landings

ROLL CAGE: metal tubing that surrounds and protects the cab in case of a rollover

ENGINE: powers the truck

DRIVER'S SEAT: where the driver sits

WHAT MAKES IT A MONSTER TRUCK?

Monster trucks are designed to be big, sturdy, and safe. But its size is what makes a monster truck special. Monster trucks are big. They are built to be powerful, to drive over other cars, and to do stunts.

Monster trucks are made to crash and land hard. Driver safety is a top priority. Over the years, safety features on monster trucks have improved. Safety begins with a strong chassis. The chassis is like the skeleton or frame of the truck. Each monster truck is built individually. But a few companies have started building standard monster truck chassis that can be used by any builder. A monster truck can then be finished with a separately made fiberglass body. The body can be unique to the truck. It is attached to the chassis.

A monster truck flips onto its roof at a Monster Jam event.

Most monster trucks have a truck engine that has been supercharged. An extra belt or a chain is attached to the engine's crankshaft, which increases the air pressure inside. The engine gets more oxygen, so it can burn more fuel, making it more powerful than engines without supercharge.

MONSTER TRUCK TRIVIA

The bodies of early monster trucks were made of sheet metal. In 1990, Bob Chandler started using fiberglass instead. Fiberglass weighs less. It's also easier to repair or replace.

Monster trucks are known for their huge tires. The standard size is 66 inches (168 cm) tall. That's taller than some people!

MONSTER TRUCK SPECS

- **Average cost to build a monster truck:** Approximately $300,000
- **Standard tire size:** 66 inches (168 cm)
- **Average height:** 10.5 feet (3 m)
- **Average weight:** 12,000 pounds (5,543 kg)
- **Average length:** 17 feet (5 m)

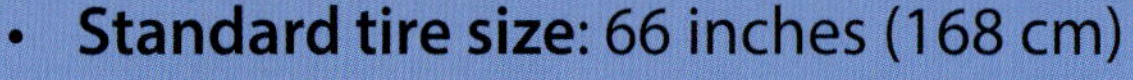
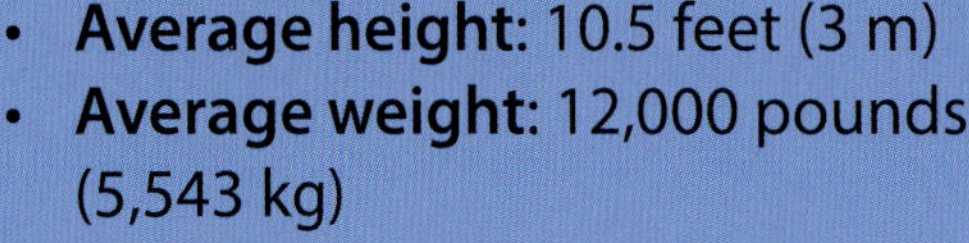

FUN FACT
A Monster Jam tire and wheel
weigh 645 pounds (293 kg)!

SAFETY FEATURES

Trucks are built with many safety features and tools to protect the driver. In 1989, USHRA set a rule that every truck had to be built with a roll cage. Within that roll cage, the driver is strapped into a harness that has five different attachment points. The harness also has points that connect to the driver's helmet. All of these parts hold the driver in place, so that even if the truck shakes, spins, or crashes into another truck, the driver doesn't move.

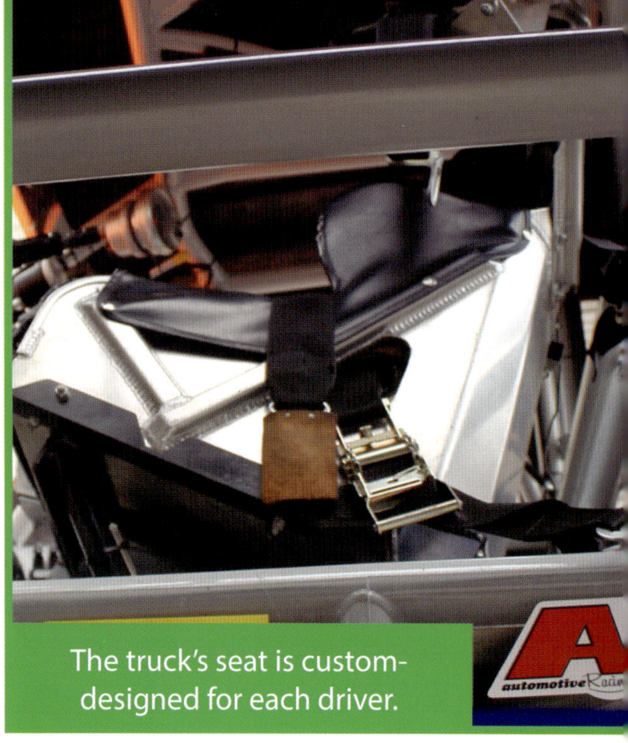

The truck's seat is custom-designed for each driver.

FUN FACT

At a Monster Jam show, the first several rows of seats stay empty. This helps to keep the audience safe.

Monster trucks get ready to compete at the Monster Jam World Finals.

Every monster truck has a fire extinguisher inside.

All of the tools and gadgets a driver needs must be within reach. This includes multiple on-off switches, so drivers can turn off a truck in a hurry. But what if a driver can't turn it off? That's a job for the remote ignition interrupter. This switch makes it possible to turn off a monster truck engine from outside of the truck. The vehicle can be turned off if the driver is hurt and can't turn it off on their own. The remote ignition interrupter was developed by Bob Chandler and a monster truck tech director named George Carpenter.

FUN FACT

Supercharging an engine not only makes it more powerful. It also makes it much louder.

MODIFICATIONS

Modifying a monster truck is what makes it special. There are three main things that are modified on a monster truck: the engine, the body style, and the design.

A monster truck has a stronger engine than other trucks. This strength is measured in a unit called horsepower (hp). A normal pickup truck has between 280 and 700 hp. Most monster trucks have a horsepower of about 1,500.

Many monster trucks start as Ford or Chevrolet pickup trucks. Their owners build them up from there. Some trucks use bodies from classic trucks. Others are custom-made to look a certain way. Paint and design are important too. They, along with the body, make each truck special.

A few early monster trucks had bigger tires than today's trucks. They were 73 inches (185 cm) tall. Just one of those tires weighed 1,050 pounds (476 kg).

AVENGER

Avenger and its driver, Jim Koehler, are part of a monster truck company called Team Scream. They have been part of every single Monster Jam World Finals event. Avenger has often been voted a fan favorite at monster truck events. Avenger is so popular that Hot Wheels made a toy version of it.

The first version of Avenger was built from a pickup truck. But in 2002, Koehler rebuilt Avenger from a 1957 Chevy Bel Air. The Bel Air was known for being a "hot rod," which means it was extra fast and accelerated quickly. People who collect classic cars still love the '57 Bel Air.

During most of its career, Avenger has been decorated with skulls and flames. One skull is on the hood, and two more are on the truck's sides. Some flames flow from the skulls, and others flow along the sides of the truck. Since 2004, Avenger has gotten a new paint style every year.

TRUCK STATS

- **Year Built**: 1996
- **Body Style**: 1957 Chevrolet Bel Air (since 2002)
- **Engine**: 575 cubic inches (9.4 l) blown Chevrolet big block
- **Awards**: World Freestyle Champion, 2003 and 2011

FUN FACT

Driver Jim Koehler named Avenger after a car his dad used to drag race.

BEARFOOT

Bearfoot was built in 1979. The earliest versions of this monster were built from a Chevy truck. The original Bearfoot weighed 18,000 pounds (8,165 kg). Around 1990, owner and driver Fred Shafer was working on Bearfoot version 10. The 10 was made of fiberglass and only weighed 8,000 pounds (3,269 kg). The 572ci motor he had used for earlier versions was too powerful for a truck that small. So he used a smaller 557ci motor for number 10.

After years of Bearfoot being a blue Chevy Silverado, Shafer switched to a red Dodge Dakota in 1992. In 1997, Fred Shafer sold the name and rights to Bearfoot to Paul Shafer. They're not related, even though they have the same last name. In 1996, Bearfoot broke the record for having the farthest distance jumped indoors and the farthest distance jumped outdoors by a monster truck.

TRUCK STATS

- **Year Built**: 1979
- **Body Style**: Chevy Silverado (1979 to 1992), Dodge Dakota (1992 to 1993), Dodge Ram (1993 to 1997)
- **Engine**: 557ci (9.5 l) Dodge/Keith Black (Bearfoot Racer #10, 1991)
- **Awards**: USHRA Camel Mud and Monster Truck World Championship 1990, 1992; USHRA Monster Wars 1993; USHRA Monster Jam World Finals 1999

The truck was retired in 1997, but a new owner bought the rights to use the Bearfoot name in 2022. Bearfoot is back on the scene with a new body and driver!

Big Crunch's theme song was "We're Not Gonna Take It" by Twisted Sister.

BIG CRUNCH

Big Crunch was a truck from Winder, Georgia. It started as a 2001 Ford F-350. Before it became Big Crunch, it was a bright red monster truck called Terrorizer. Owner Michael Hawes sold it to Tom Schmidt around 2004. Schmidt owned and drove the truck until 2012, when it was retired.

In its first years, Big Crunch was red, with a black-and-white logo and a red-and-white checked pattern toward the back. Later on, the logo changed to silver and yellow, with a blue wave behind it. The final version of Big Crunch was bright blue, with a yellow front bumper, orange flames, and red, white, and blue logo.

TRUCK STATS

- **Year Built**: 2004
- **Body Style**: 2001 Ford F-350 Super Duty
- **Engine**: 460ci (7.5 l) Ford V-8

Lots of engine descriptions include the abbreviation "ci." That stands for cubic inches. This measures how much space in the engine can fill with air and fuel. The higher an engine's ci number, the more air and fuel it can take in and burn. This means the engine is more powerful.

BIGFOOT

Bigfoot is known as the first monster truck. When Bob Chandler built it in the 1970s, no one was even using the name "monster truck" yet. An announcer coined the term in 1981, at one of Bigfoot's first shows. The first Bigfoot weighed 11,000 pounds (4,990 kg) and had 48-inch (122 cm) tires. In 1982, Bigfoot 2 was built with 66-inch (168 cm) tires.

TRUCK STATS

- **Year Built**: 1974
- **Body Style**: Ford F-250 (Bigfoot 1)
- **Engine**: 460ci (7.5 l) Big Block V-8 (Bigfoot 1)

FUN FACT

Bob Chandler's wife, Marilyn, was the first female monster truck driver. But she didn't compete.

Bigfoot got its name from a mechanic. Even in the early days, Bigfoot always needed repairs because of Chandler's hard driving. The mechanic told Chandler he had a big foot that was always on the gas pedal. The name stuck. People were so excited about the huge truck that Chandler and Bigfoot started traveling to events around the country. During its busiest years, Bigfoot drove at more than 1,000 events each year.

Bigfoot competes in a monster truck show in 2024.

Chandler was always interested in making Bigfoot better and safer. He was the first to make many changes that were later made to other monster trucks. Bigfoot 23 came out in 2023.

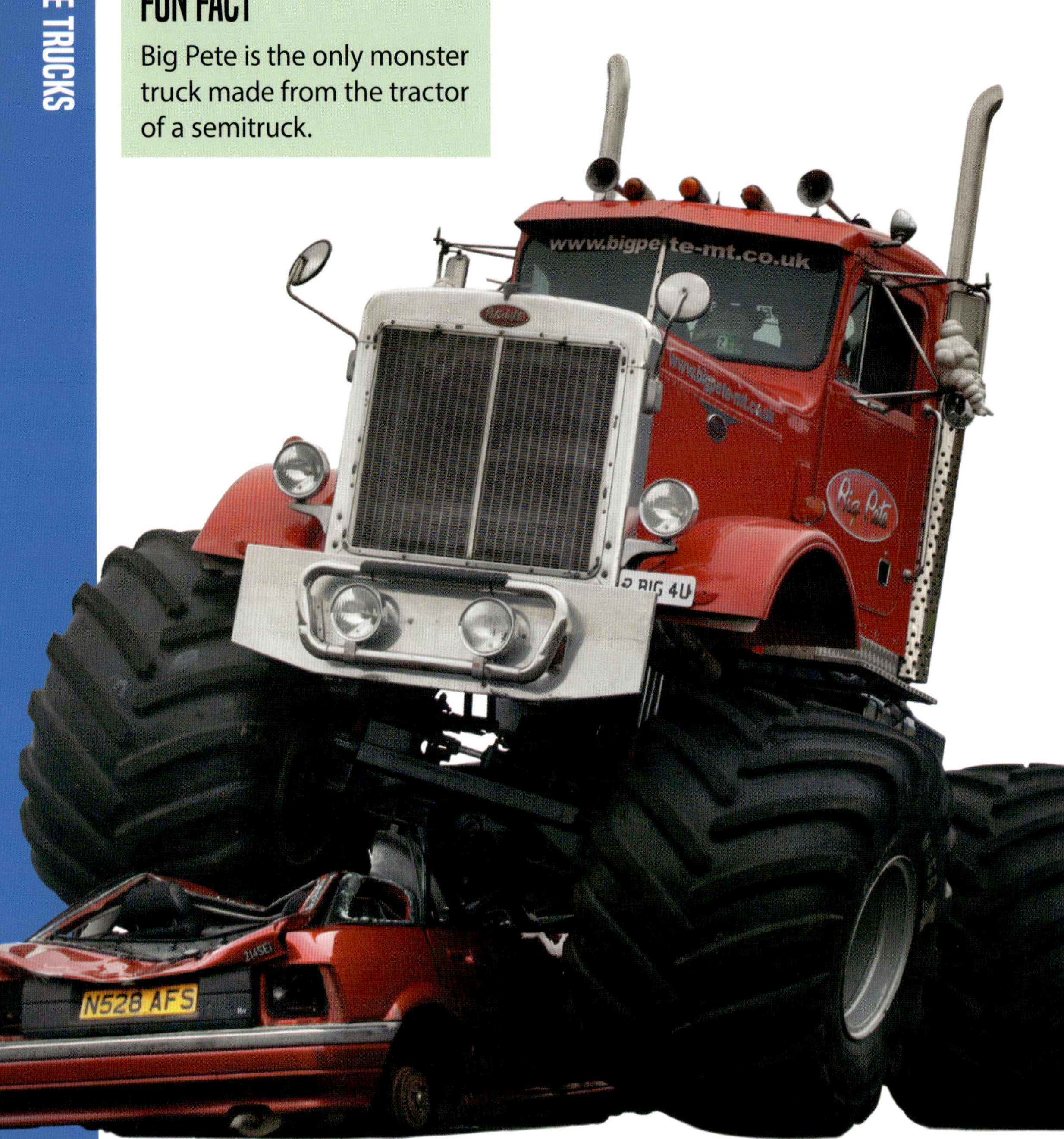

FUN FACT

Big Pete is the only monster truck made from the tractor of a semitruck.

BIG PETE

Most monster trucks are built in the United States, but Big Pete comes from England. Its hometown is Hebden Bridge, in West Yorkshire. The company Big Pete Ltd. owns this truck, along with its teammate Grim Reaper. Company owner Mike Murty drives Big Pete. The trucks and their crew travel around the United Kingdom, from Scotland to Northern Ireland to Wales.

TRUCK STATS

- **Year Built**: 2002
- **Body Style**: Peterbilt 359
- **Engine**: 454ci (7.4 l) Chevrolet V-8

Big Pete is made from a semitruck. It even has a removable monster trailer. Big Pete and its trailer were designed to be able to crush cars just as well as any other monster truck.

Suspension is the system in a vehicle that holds the tires, axles, and body together. Big Pete is one of the only monster trucks to use leaf-spring suspension. This kind of suspension was developed way back in the 18th century. It works, but riding in the truck is bumpy. It's also rougher on the truck's body. Newer systems make the ride feel smoother. Big Pete's team replaces the springs at least twice a year.

BLACK STALLION

Black Stallion has been around longer than most monster trucks. Its look has changed over the years, though. Its driver, Michael Vaters, built the first Black Stallion in 1981. At first, Black Stallion wasn't a competitive monster truck. It could drive on streets. Later, Vaters built it into a monster truck. Black Stallion competed with other trucks at car-crushing events. Soon, it joined monster truck competitions at small arenas.

In 1996, Vaters rebuilt Black Stallion. He called the new version Black Stallion 2000. In 1999, Black Stallion was the first monster truck to jump over another monster truck without crashing. That same year, Black Stallion won its first championship at the Thunder Nationals. A few years later, it would take the same title three years in a row. The truck has appeared in four monster truck video games. Black Stallion has competed in five Monster Jam Finals. But it has yet to win.

FUN FACT

Thunder Nationals events didn't use big piles of dirt in its arenas. Trucks crushed cars, raced, and did stunts.

TRUCK STATS

- **Year Built**: 1981
- **Body Style**: 2008 Ford F-150
- **Engine**: 540ci (8.8 l) Ford Performance
- **Awards**: Thunder Nationals Champion: 1999, 2005, 2006, 2007

During a 2001 race, Black Stallion's forward gear stopped working. So Vaters competed in reverse! He later became known for doing stunts in reverse. In fact, Vaters holds the world record for farthest jump in reverse. He jumped Black Stallion 70 feet (21 m) in 2002.

BLUE THUNDER

Driver Lyle Hancock and Blue Thunder debuted at the Houston Astrodome in January 2001. After that first event, Monster Jam invited Blue Thunder to its finals. That would be the first of 17 appearances at this event. Even though Blue Thunder is an official Monster Jam truck, it has never been a Monster Jam champion.

Every version of Blue Thunder has a lightning bolt pattern on its bright blue paint job. But each pattern looks different. It has been a very popular monster truck since its debut in 2001.

TRUCK STATS

- **Year Built**: 2001
- **Body Style**: 2008 Ford F-150 (since 2013)
- **Engine**: 540ci (8.8 l) Merlin (2001 to 2016, 2022 to present)

MONSTER TRUCK TRIVIA

Blue Thunder has shown up in 10 video games. The fast-food restaurants McDonald's, Burger King, and Wendy's have all offered toy Blue Thunder trucks with kids' meals. Hot Wheels makes a toy version too.

Blue Thunder toy

During its long career, Blue Thunder has had 25 different drivers.

BOUNTY HUNTER

Before Bounty Hunter was Bounty Hunter, it was a truck called Shark Attack. Driver and owner Jimmy Creten started Bounty Hunter's career at small shows in the Midwest. Creten soon bought another truck and turned it into a second Bounty Hunter. Since then, his Kansas-based company, 2Xtreme Racing, has grown to three trucks.

TRUCK STATS

- **Year Built**: 1995
- **Body Style**: Ford Expedition (since 2002)
- **Engine**: 55ci (0.9 l) Blown Alcohol
- **Awards**: 2015 No Limits Monster Truck Champion, 2019 World Finals Racing Champion

Bounty Hunter

Bounty Hunter competes at the Monster Truck Nationals.

Jimmy Creten's wife, Dawn Creten, is also a monster truck driver. She usually drives a truck called Scarlet Bandit, also owned by 2Xtreme Racing. She has driven the company's other truck, Iron Outlaw, as well. Dawn and Scarlet Bandit have appeared in three Monster Jam World Finals. She is considered one of the most famous female monster truck drivers.

Bounty Hunter competed in 18 Monster Jam World Finals events. The first one was in 2002.

FUN FACT

The cartoon character Yosemite Sam was painted on the very first version of Bounty Hunter.

CAPTAIN AMERICA

In 2012, Marvel Comics and Feld Motorsports began a partnership. Together, they made monster trucks that looked like Marvel Comics heroes.

Feld's Captain America truck was based on the Marvel Comics character of the same name. As part of the same partnership, Marvel Comics also had a Wolverine monster truck. Captain America and

TRUCK STATS

- **Year Built**: 2012
- **Body Style**: Custom-Made 3D Concept
- **Engine**: 540ci (8.8 l) Merlin

MONSTER TRUCK TRIVIA

After a run in the Captain America truck, Fortune liked to pose with a Captain America shield. At some shows, he gave away the shield to a lucky audience member. When he drove Superman, he often started performing his show outside the truck, dressed as Clark Kent.

Chad Fortune, Captain America's driver

Captain America competes
at Monster Jam in 2014.

its driver Chad Fortune made it to the Monster Jam World Finals three years in a row, from 2012 to 2014.

Chad Fortune was no stranger to driving superhero-themed trucks. Before Captain America, he had driven DC Comics' truck Superman. Fortune and Superman drove together from 2005 to 2012. But even before he drove a monster truck at all, Fortune had other jobs. He was both a professional football player and a professional wrestler.

CRUSHER

Crusher started out its career in Great Britain in 2009. But before it was Crusher, the truck performed under the name Monstrous.

Crusher and its driver Lewis Cook might be best known for a stunt back in 2011. They were competing in a Monster Truck Nationals event in Northamptonshire, England. Cook was driving Crusher through a 90-second freestyle run. The course had a few obstacles, including a bus and a fire truck. Cook launched Crusher, intending to jump the fire truck. But instead, Crusher got stuck on its back wheels with its nose in the air! After six minutes of being stuck, emergency crews used a crane to set Crusher free.

TRUCK STATS

- **Year Built**: 2009
- **Body Style**: Ford F-150/ Dodge Ram
- **Engine**: 540ci (8.8 l) Merlin

FUN FACT

The kids' show *Blaze and the Monster Machines* has a character called Crusher. But that cartoon Crusher isn't related to the real-life Crusher.

CRUSHSTATION

Crushstation's nickname is "the Monstah Lobstah." Crushstation and its driver, Greg Winchenbach, come from the state of Maine, which produces more lobsters than any other state. Winchenbach even named his monster truck company Bottom Feeder Motorsports. Bottom feeders are certain types of fish and shellfish, like lobsters, that eat food from the bottom of the ocean. Crushstation is designed to look like a bright red lobster. Its artwork even includes a picture of a scared lobster harvester!

TRUCK STATS

- **Year Built**: 2009
- **Body Style**: Custom-Built Lobster
- **Engine**: 540 Merlin/585ci (9.6 l) Chevrolet Blown and Alcohol Injected
- **Awards**: Monster Truck Throwdown Champion, 2015 and 2016; 2018 Traxxas Monster Truck Champion

MONSTER TRUCK TRIVIA

The name Crushstation comes from the word *crustacean*. That's a type of animal that has an exoskeleton and antennae. Lobsters are one kind of crustacean. So are shrimp, crabs, and wood lice.

DEFENDER

The yellow-and-red monster truck Defender comes from Indiana. It's often called by its full name, Rislone Defender. That's because it's sponsored by a company called Rislone, which makes a substance used in car tune-ups. Defender was decorated with flames and a mad scientist on the side.

Greg Adams and his son Zach Adams owned and drove the truck. As Zach was growing up, he spent a lot of time in the garage, watching his dad repair, build, and drive trucks. He got an early, hands-on education on monster truck mechanics and driving.

TRUCK STATS

- **Year Built**: 2008
- **Body Style**: Ford Raptor
- **Engine**: 540ci (8.8 l)

FUN FACT

Defender and other monster trucks don't drive to their own events. They ride in a trailer. Defender's transport trailer is 53 feet (16 m) long and 8.5 feet (3 m) wide.

Zach started driving in 2008 when he was 22. He quickly became the 2009 MTRA Rookie of the Year. Since he started driving, he's won at least 55 awards.

MONSTER TRUCK TRIVIA

Defender is one of more than 30 trucks featured in a video game called *Monster Truck Destruction*, which came out in 2012. Players of the game can drive and crash monster trucks of their choice, just as real-life drivers do.

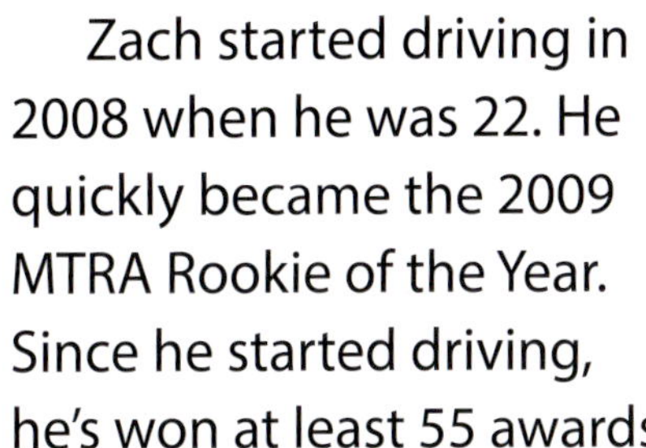

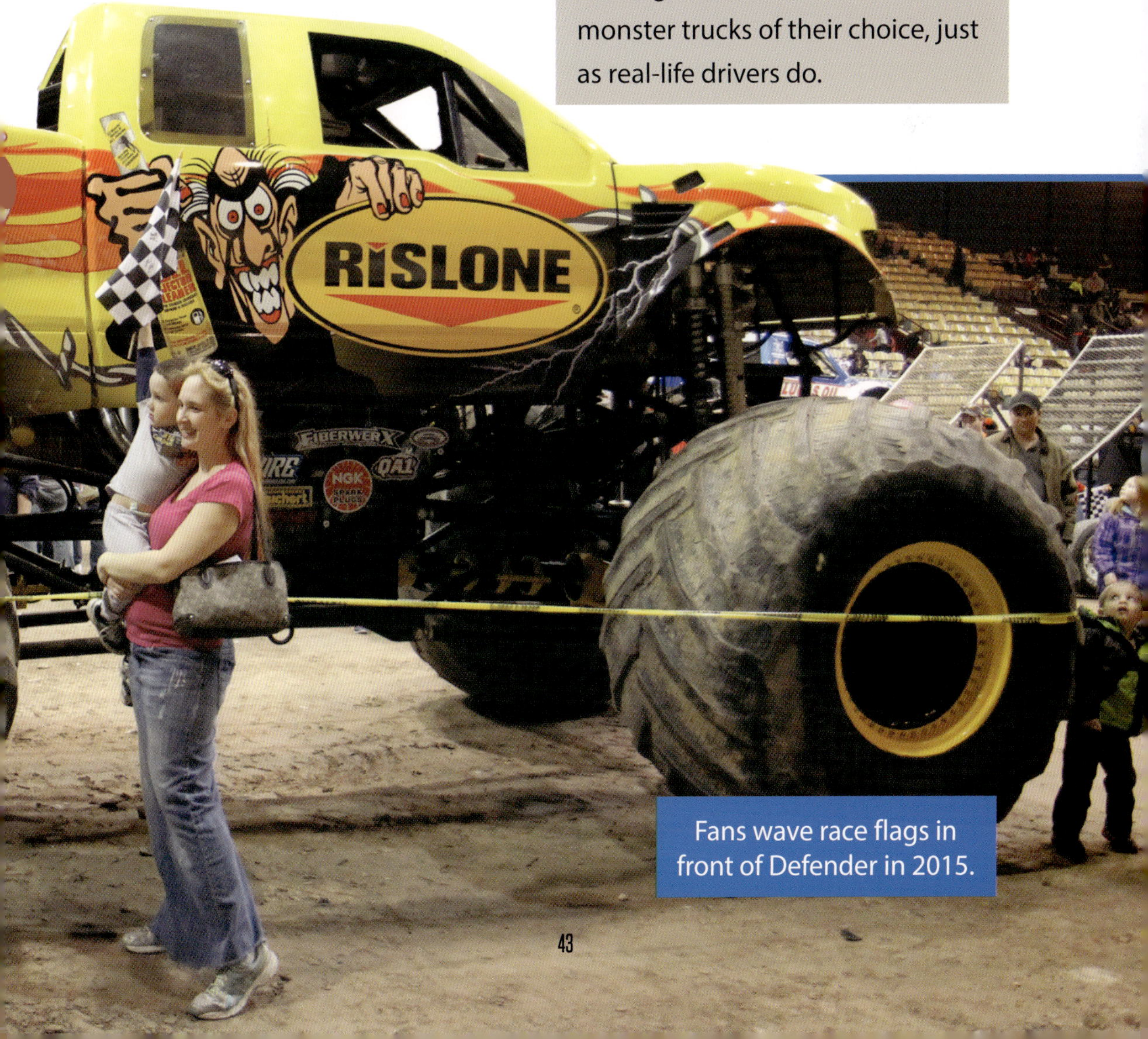

Fans wave race flags in front of Defender in 2015.

DESTROYER

Dan Evans built Destroyer in 1999. The first version of Destroyer had previously been known as Blue Max. It stayed blue for a little while, but the next year, Evans built a new version of Destroyer. The new body was red. Destroyer and Evans were invited to the Monster Jam World Finals in 2001.

In 2002, Evans began performing freestyle moves in reverse. Soon, he would become well-known for this reverse move. Destroyer's body was destroyed after the 2007 freestyle competition of the Monster Jam World Finals. It had to be rebuilt.

In 2011, Dan Evans started driving for Feld Motorsports, which owns Monster Jam. He sold Destroyer to Roger Stidell.

TRUCK STATS

- **Year Built**: 1999
- **Body Style**: 1992 Chevrolet C/K (1999); 1999 Chevrolet S10 (2000 to 2007); 2007 Ford F-150 (2007 to 2012); Custom Ford Trophy Truck (since 2013)
- **Engine**: 540ci (8.8 l) Merlin

MONSTER TRUCK TRIVIA

Monster trucks and video games are a fun combination. Fans can race their favorite trucks and do stunts. Destroyer has appeared in five different monster truck video games.

Destroyer does a ramp jump.

Stidell drove Destroyer for five years. A 2016 Monster Jam show in Oakland, California, was the last time Destroyer performed in public. During its career, Destroyer and driver Dan Evans made it to the Monster Jam World Finals six times!

FUN FACT

In 2007, Evans rebuilt Destroyer from a new Ford F-150.

Earth Shaker competes at Monster Jam in Massachusetts.

EARTH SHAKER

Earth Shaker was introduced in 2017. It looks like a dump truck. Its style honors machines, trucks, and construction workers everywhere.

Driver Tristan England and Earth Shaker made a name for themselves right away by winning the Double Down Showdown at Monster Jam World Finals XVIII. There have been several versions of Earth Shaker. With different drivers and different trucks, Earth Shaker has traveled the world.

Earth Shaker is part of a toy franchise called Monster Jam Truckin' Pals. The Earth Shaker toy truck is able to create the dirt tracks the trucks run on. And it can tear up those tracks too.

TRUCK STATS

- **Year Built**: 2017
- **Body Style**: Custom Dump Truck Concept
- **Engine**: 540ci (8.8 l) Merlin
- **Awards**: 2017 Double Down Showdown Champion; Monster Jam Triple Threat Series Champion 2018 and 2019; 2023 Monster Jam World Finals Racing Champion

FUN FACT

A toy version of the truck includes a pile of dirt in the truck's bed.

EL TORO LOCO

The name El Toro Loco means "the Crazy Bull" in Spanish. Monster Jam introduced the truck in 2001. It was a Spanish spin-off of a truck called Bulldozer. From the beginning, fans loved El Toro Loco. By 2012, there were four El Toro Loco trucks that could travel to events. In 2018, the El Toro Loco team had seven trucks!

By 2013, El Toro Loco had three different color designs for the trucks: orange, yellow, and black. This changed over the years, but at least one truck is always orange. Some versions of the truck have a nose ring or a gold tooth.

MONSTER TRUCK TRIVIA

One of El Toro Loco's design features is a nose on its hood that blows smoke. Some drivers use the feature to snort at their biggest rivals.

FUN FACT

Hot Wheels made a toy version of El Toro Loco.

El Toro Loco has competed in every Monster Jam World Finals event since 2003. With so many trucks and so many competitions, 56 different drivers have driven El Toro Loco over the years.

GAS MONKEY GARAGE

Monster Jam made the monster truck known as Gas Monkey Garage especially for a TV show. *Fast N' Loud* was a reality show on the Discovery Channel that aired from 2012 to 2020. It followed a Texas auto shop called Gas Monkey Garage. The mechanics at the shop did custom work on cars for customers. They focused on classic cars and hot rods.

TRUCK STATS

- **Year Built**: 2016
- **Body Style**: 1970 Dodge Coronet Super Bee
- **Engine**: 540ci (8.8 l) Merlin

FUN FACT

A single truck participates in a show for up to 15 minutes. But getting ready for that event takes a truck's team about 60 hours!

Monster Jam owned the monster truck version of Gas Monkey Garage. Its main driver was BJ Johnson. When he was not driving, Joe Sylvester and Lynsey Weenk sometimes filled in for him. Gas Monkey Garage, with BJ Johnson driving, made it to the Monster Jam World Finals three times, but it never won.

Gas Monkey Garage races in Brazil.

MONSTER TRUCK TRIVIA

Engine strength is measured in units called horsepower. A long time ago, people compared the power of an engine to the strength of horses, which were used to do work such as pulling plows or carriages. The higher an engine's horsepower, the more powerful it is.

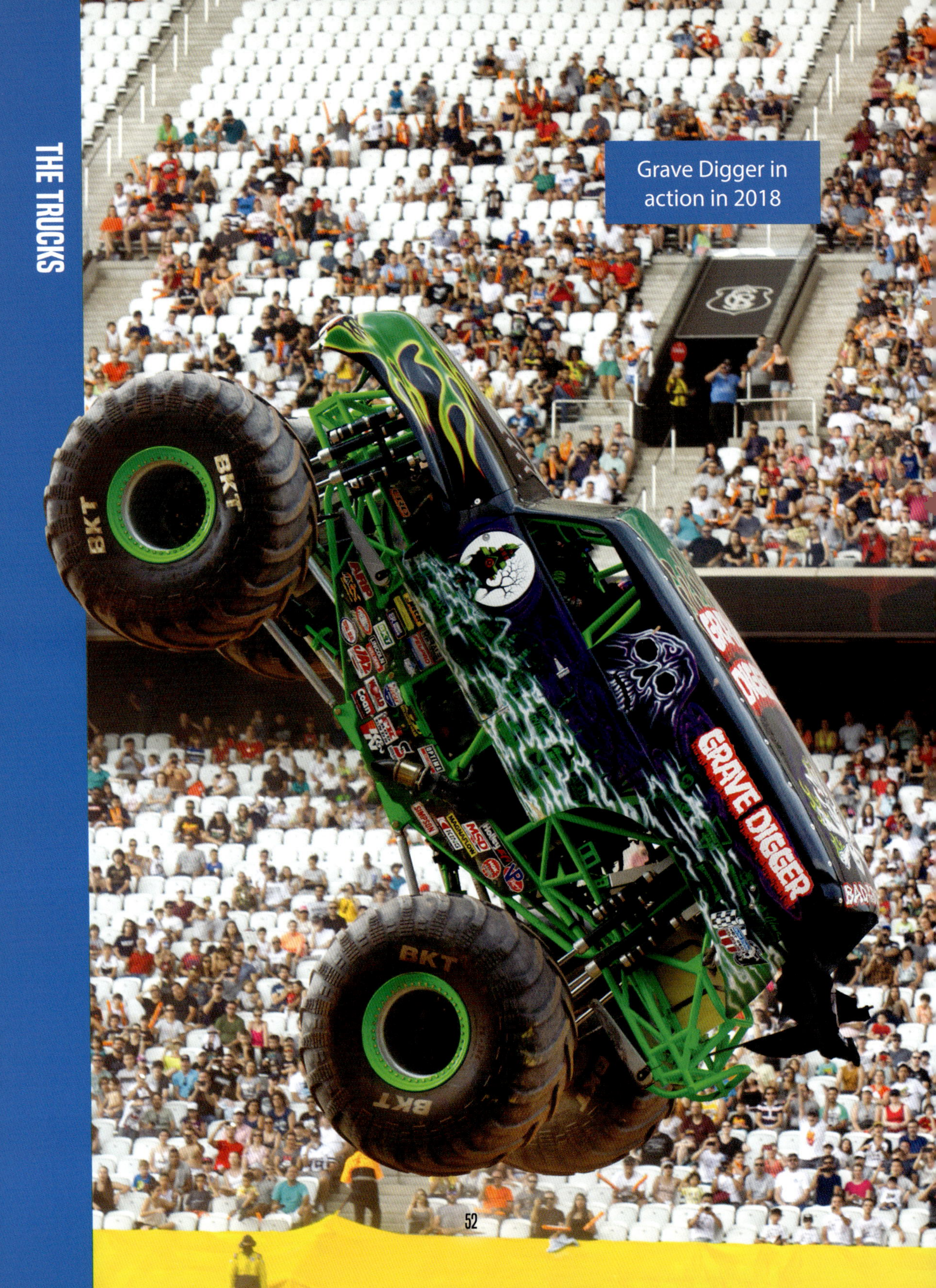

Grave Digger in action in 2018

GRAVE DIGGER

Grave Digger is known as the second monster truck in history. It's also one of the most famous. Dennis Anderson is the truck's driver and builder. Back in 1982, he and his friends would put tractor tires on trucks and drive through mud. Anderson added parts from a junkyard and old tractors to a 1952 Ford pickup. The truck became the famous Grave Digger.

Grave Digger's name came from an argument. A wealthy kid was giving Anderson a hard time about using old parts. Anderson said, "I will take this junk and dig you a grave." The name stuck.

Over the next few decades, the Grave Digger business grew. In 2012, Anderson's children were old enough to start driving. Today, all four of them drive monster trucks. Grave Digger celebrated its 40th anniversary in 2022, and it has had more than 40 official Grave Digger trucks over the years. It takes about 60 hours to build a Grave Digger truck.

TRUCK STATS

- **Year Built**: 1982
- **Body Style**: 1951 Chevrolet Panel Van
- **Engine**: 540ci (8.8 l) Merlin
- **Awards**: Monster Jam World Finals Racing, 2004, 2006, 2010, 2016, 2018, and 2022; Monster Jam World Finals Freestyle, 2000 and 2016

MONSTER TRUCK TRIVIA

Monster truck drivers and owners often choose theme songs to play while a truck enters an arena. In its early years, the song "Bad to the Bone" by George Thorogood and the Destroyers played when Grave Digger started its shows.

GRIM REAPER

Grim Reaper started out in 1996 as a truck called Blown Thunder, in Georgia. Then, in 2003, its owner sold the truck to a company called Extreme Machines, in Suffolk, England. Two years later, the company Big Pete Ltd. bought the truck and turned it into Grim Reaper. The company also owns the truck known as Big Pete.

MONSTER TRUCK TRIVIA

Grim Reaper and Big Pete often perform together. The two are known for a stunt in which they play tug-of-war with a junk car. The trucks are so strong, they tear the junk car in half!

Grim Reaper and its teammate Big Pete mostly perform outdoors on grass. Other monster trucks usually drive on dirt floor arenas.

TRUCK STATS

- **Year Built**: 2006
- **Body Style**: 1999 Chevrolet Silverado
- **Engine**: Big Block Chevrolet V-8

Gunslinger takes off during a competition.

GUNSLINGER

Scott Hartsock started driving Gunslinger in 1992. Before that, he did a lot of hunting. He also designed and worked on firearms. Hartsock called himself a gunslinger. That's where the truck's name came from.

Fan favorite Gunslinger made it to the World Finals seven times. But it missed the freestyle competition at three of those. That's a record, but maybe not a good one. At one event, Gunslinger crashed into a wall during the racing part. And at the other two, Hartsock drove so hard he broke the truck's engine!

In 2016, Monster Jam made a new rule. They wouldn't allow guns in relation to monster trucks in Monster Jam events. That meant Gunslinger couldn't compete at Monster Jam any more. But the truck still made appearances at other events.

TRUCK STATS

- **Year Built**: 1992
- **Body Style**: Ford F-150 (1992–2004); Chevrolet Silverado (2005–2006); Ford F-150 Trophy Truck (since 2013)
- **Engine**: 557ci (8.8 l) SVO Blown Ford

MONSTER TRUCK TRIVIA

After the name Gunslinger wasn't allowed at Monster Jam, the team made a new version of the truck called Slinger.

IRON MAN

In 2010, Feld Motorsports debuted Iron Man. The truck was modeled on the Marvel comic book character of the same name. At the same time, the company also had a Spider-Man monster truck. The early version of Iron Man made it to the World Finals five times. Iron Man competed for four years, until the end of Feld's contract with Marvel. In 2023, Feld and Marvel signed a new contract and launched a new version of Iron Man. Its new Marvel teammates were Black Panther, Thor, and Spider-Man.

TRUCK STATS

- **Year Built**: 2010
- **Body Style**: 2010 Custom Mark VI (2010 to 2014); 2023 Custom Mark VI
- **Engine**: 540ci (8.8 l) Merlin

MONSTER TRUCK TRIVIA

Monster trucks and superheroes go well together. Marvel's monster trucks are based on their Avengers characters. Iron Man is one of the most popular trucks.

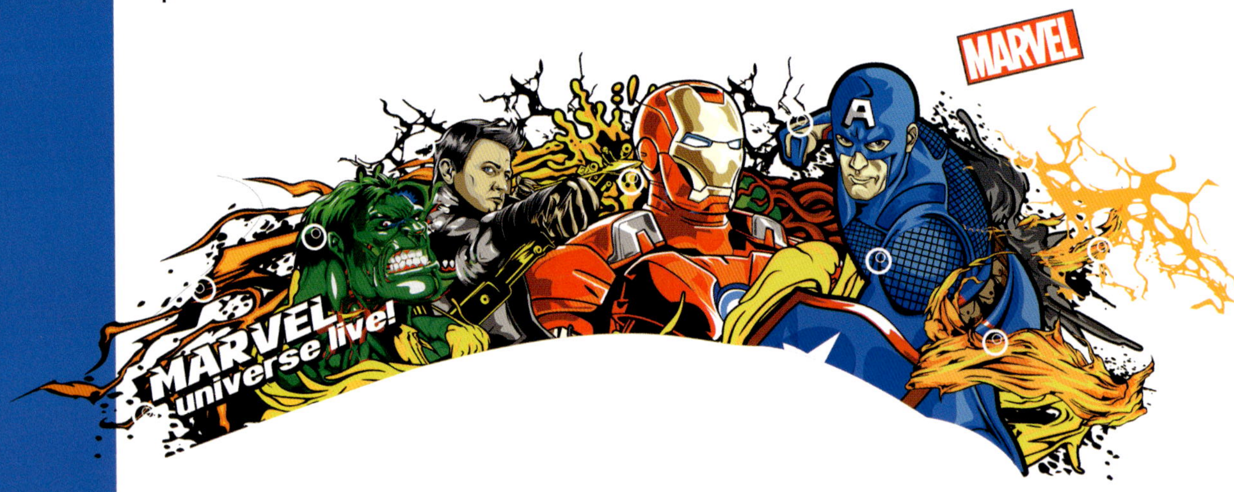

The main driver of Iron Man was Lee O'Donnell. But four other drivers drove the truck as well. O'Donnell drove monster trucks from 1999 to 2018, when he retired. He won the 2017 freestyle championship at the Monster Jam World Finals, but not in Iron Man! He was also the first driver to do a barrel roll and a front flip during competition.

IRON OUTLAW

Driver Linsey Weenk was the first to show off Iron Outlaw in 2005. Before driving monster trucks, Weenk was a hockey player. Just one year after their debut, Weenk and Iron Outlaw won 21 races in a row. The team was so impressive that Monster Jam invited them to the World Finals in Las Vegas, where they were named rising stars.

The monster truck team 2Xtreme Racing owns Iron Outlaw. Its best-known teammates are Bounty Hunter and Scarlet Bandit. 2Xtreme Racing's owners, Dawn and Jimmy Creten, are well-known in the monster truck world. Not only do they own the company, but they also both drive monster trucks themselves.

TRUCK STATS

- **Year Built**: 2005
- **Body Style**: 2005 Ford Expedition
- **Engine**: 540ci (8.8 l) Blown Alcohol

MONSTER TRUCK TRIVIA

Iron Outlaw has used some different identities over the years. It has been called Outlaw, Scarlet Bandit, and Monster Mutt, to name a few. In 2020, the truck known as Iron Outlaw started going by the name Hot Tamale.

FUN FACT

Over its lifetime, Iron Outlaw has had 30 different drivers.

TRUCK STATS

- **Year Built**: 1999
- **Body Style**: Custom-Built Triceratops
- **Engine**: 540ci (8.8 l) Chevrolet
- **Awards**: 2008 Monster Jam Save of the Year; 2021 Nashville Monster Jam Freestyle Winner; 2022 Toughest Monster Truck Tour Winner

JURASSIC ATTACK

A Canadian driver named Don Frankish launched the original Jurassic Attack in 1999. He was inspired by the truck Snake Bite. Snake Bite, which came onto the scene in 1991, was the first monster truck with a custom-built hood that had a 3D body. Over the years, Jurassic Attack became so popular that Frankish built a version that could take people for a ride, but not in a competition, of course!

In 2011, Frankish and Jurassic Attack took a long break. But in 2021, Team Throttle Monster bought the name and kicked off a new career for the truck. The team owns several other monster trucks and brought Jurassic Attack back in style. The team's Dalton Widner usually drives the truck.

In 2007 and 2008, Jurassic Attack started some of its events in a cage. It stayed there while other trucks were introduced. Then the cage would open to release the truck for attack.

Lil' Devil in 2011

LIL' DEVIL

Lil' Devil was part of a UK company called Extreme Events Europe Ltd. Before it became Lil' Devil, the truck was called The Rock. But in 2003, it was sold and moved to England. The new team rebuilt the truck, and it won the Monster Truck Racing Association competition in 2004. The first version of Lil' Devil was black, but most later versions have been red.

Lil' Devil became a TV personality, appearing in shows in the United Kingdom, including *Men & Motors* and *The Race*. The truck kept competing, and occasionally Lil' Devil performed under the name Super Charger. Its driver, Ian Batey, owned other monster trucks too. Before Batey drove Lil' Devil, he did other kinds of stunt shows, including motorcycle jumps and human cannons. He started his career at 16 years old. He later taught himself how to repair cars.

Super Charger

FUN FACT

Lil' Devil hasn't officially retired, but it hasn't been competing in recent years.

TRUCK STATS

- **Year Built**: 2003
- **Body Style**: Chevrolet Silverado
- **Engine**: 540ci (8.8 l) Chevrolet
- **Awards**: 2004 MTRA Winner; 2010 Guinness World Record for Can Crushing

MADUSA

Madusa's driver was also nicknamed Madusa. Her real name is Debrah Miceli. Before she became a monster truck driver, Miceli was a professional wrestler. Madusa the truck has a wrestling-themed design.

Madusa the truck competed in the Monster Jam World Finals 14 times. Madusa and Debrah Miceli's 2005 Monster Jam Racing Championship was the first time a female driver won a monster truck world championship. Madusa drove for Monster Jam until 2006. Then the truck took a break while Miceli drove for a different team, but both truck and driver came back to Monster Jam in 2009.

TRUCK STATS

- **Year Built**: 2000
- **Body Style**: Ford F-150
- **Engine**: 540ci (8.8 l) Merlin
- **Awards**: 2004 Monster Jam World Finals Freestyle Co-Champion; 2005 Monster Jam World Finals Racing Championship

MONSTER TRUCK TRIVIA

The name Madusa is short for "made in the USA." It's also a play on the name Medusa, a monster in Greek mythology.

Miceli and Madusa planned to retire in 2017. But Miceli couldn't compete in 2016 or 2017 because of injuries. She did come back for part of 2020 to drive in Australia.

Madusa's driver, Debrah Miceli, holds the Guinness World Record for being the first female driver to compete at Monster Jam.

MARTIAL LAW

Martial Law and its owner and driver Paul Strong are from Minnesota. Strong started driving monster trucks in 2006, when he built Martial Law. In 2009, he and his wife, Kaila Savage, built a truck called Heart Breaker. It would be a teammate to Martial Law. Savage, driving Heart Breaker, was the first female driver to land a backflip in a monster truck.

Early in its career, Martial Law was painted blue and white, with a simple swirl design. Later on, it had a green background with a tough-looking sheriff on the side.

Strong was known for being a wild driver and for racing hard. Martial Law retired in 2012, but Strong kept the truck. He began driving other monster trucks, including Master of Disaster.

TRUCK STATS

- **Year Built**: 2006
- **Body Style**: 2005 Ford F-150
- **Engine**: 475 Ford

FUN FACT

On a 2019 Monster Jam tour, Strong drove the trucks Storm Damage and Zombie Fire.

MARTIAL
LAW

MAXIMUM DESTRUCTION-D

Maximum Destruction might be one of the biggest names in the monster truck world. It began its career in 1999, under the name Goldberg, for a wrestler in World Championship Wrestling (WCW). Driver Tom Meents built the truck, with support from WCW and PACE Motorsports. When the WCW contract ended, Tom Meents kept the truck he'd built and driven. For two years, he called the truck Team Meents.

Max-D makes a lot of jumps and takes a lot of hits during freestyle runs. But it was built to hold up in crashes.

In 2003, the truck was unleashed under its new name, Maximum Destruction. Since then, it has won the Monster Jam World Racing Championship three times and the Monster Jam World Freestyle championship four times.

TRUCK STATS

- **Year Built**: 2003
- **Body Style**: 2000 Futuristic SUV
- **Engine**: 540ci (8.8 l) Merlin
- **Awards**: Monster Jam World Finals Racing Champion: 2009, 2011, and 2012; Monster Jam World Finals Freestyle Champion: 2004, 2006, 2013, and 2022

MONSTER TRUCK TRIVIA

Max-D's engine is mounted on the front of the truck. That's different from most monster trucks, which have their engines in the middle of the truck.

Along with Tom, Colton and Jared Eichelberger are two of Max-D's regular drivers. They also happen to be Tom Meents's stepsons.

By 2013, the Maximum Destruction team had five trucks. For its 10-year anniversary, the trucks got new designs. They shared an illustration of a character called Creator of Chaos. Around this time, the team shortened the truck's name to Max-D. Over the years, there have been 10 different versions of Maximum Destruction.

MEGALODON

Megalodon monster truck is modeled after the prehistoric predator with the same name. The truck's foam fins flap around during races.

The 2017 Monster Jam World Finals was the first to include fans judging the freestyle competition. Megalodon was the first performer in this competition and the first to be judged by fans. Six years later, Megalodon had six trucks and six usual drivers competing at six different competitions.

Driver Bernard Lyght is one of a few Black monster truck drivers. He knows that young people look up to him, and he wants to be a good role model. Before Lyght started driving monster trucks, he worked as an acrobat, a cheerleader, and a stuntman. Lyght's favorite trick in driving Megalodon is the sky wheelie.

TRUCK STATS

- **Year Built**: 2017
- **Body Style**: Custom 3D Shark Concept
- **Engine**: 540ci (8.8 l) Merlin
- **Awards**: 2017 Triple Threat Series Central Champion

MONSTER TRUCK TRIVIA

The megalodon was a huge prehistoric shark—one with a mouth big enough to hold an adult human!

MEGALODON
MONSTER JAM
BKT
BKT
MONSTER
ENERG

Todd LeDuc makes a jump in Metal Mulisha at Monster Jam in Australia.

METAL MULISHA

The first driver and owner of Metal Mulisha was Brian Deegan. Before and after his monster truck career, he was a champion motocross racer. In 1997, Deegan started the clothing company Metal Mulisha. Then, in 2011, Deegan and Monster Jam announced a new truck named Metal Mulisha.

When Deegan was out with an injury, driver Todd LeDuc drove Metal Mulisha. LeDuc had been part of Metal Mulisha's off-road racing team. Another of the truck's drivers was Matt Buyten, who had driven motocross with the Metal Mulisha team.

TRUCK STATS

- **Year Built**: 2011
- **Body Style**: 2008 Ford F-150
- **Engine**: 540ci (8.8 l) Merlin
- **Awards**: Monster Jam World Freestyle Champion 2014; Monster Jam World Racing Champion 2015

MONSTER TRUCK TRIVIA

Metal Mulisha was retired in 2017. The company Metal Mulisha no longer owns a monster truck. But it still sells clothing and sponsors other motorsports.

MOHAWK WARRIOR

Mohawk Warrior can be recognized by its black mohawk hairstyle. The truck's fans call themselves Mohawk Nation.

Mohawk Warrior's first driver was George Balhan. He was popular among fans, and he was known for having a mohawk hairstyle of his own. The Mohawk Warrior truck was designed by Balhan himself. He drove other trucks as well as Mohawk Warrior, but he retired from monster trucks in 2016.

Mohawk Warrior's driver since 2017, Bryce Kenny, used to be a professional drag racer. He drives so fast that he and Mohawk Warrior set a world speed record for a monster truck. They were clocked at 100.3 miles (161 km) per hour. Kenny performs with his own hair in a mohawk to match the truck. But his mohawk isn't as distinctive as Balhan's was.

FUN FACT

Mohawk Warrior is sponsored by Great Clips, a haircut franchise.

TRUCK STATS

- **Year Built**: 2010
- **Body Style**: 2004 Cadillac Escalade
- **Engine**: 650ci (10.6 l) Merlin
- **Awards**: 2019 Monster Jam Save of the Year Award

WORLD FINA
CH 22-
MOHAWK WARRIOR
NGK
SPARK
PLUGS

MONSTER MUTT DALMATIAN

The first truck in the Monster Mutt series was simply called Monster Mutt. It debuted in 2003. It was so popular that since then, three more trucks have joined the Monster Jam dog pound. Monster Mutt Dalmatian was next. In 2007, the black-and-white spotted truck made its debut. Like the original, it has a floppy tongue, tail, and ears.

Monster Mutt Dalmatian has mostly been driven by female drivers. Two of its first drivers were Cynthia Gauthier and Candice Jolly. Jolly has been racing vehicles since she was eight years old. She started with go-karts.

TRUCK STATS

- **Year Built**: 2007
- **Body Style**: 1950 Mercury Street Rod (until 2015); Custom 3D Dog Concept (since 2016)
- **Engine**: 540ci (8.8 l) Merlin

MONSTER TRUCK TRIVIA

Monster Mutt Dalmatian has words on its underside: "Beggin' for Bones." Fans can see them when the truck does wheelies.

At the start of Monster Mutt Dalmation's races, someone throws a bone for the Mutt to chase.

Driver Colt Stephens launches Monster Mutt Rottweiler over a jump.

MONSTER MUTT ROTTWEILER

Monster Mutt Rottweiler is sometimes called Rotty for short. It is the third truck in the group of monster trucks known as Monster Mutts. Rotty got its start at a fan contest. Fans suggested names for new Monster Mutt trucks, and Rottweiler was the winner. Feld Entertainment, the company that owns Monster Jam, owns and manages this truck. At least 15 different drivers have driven Monster Mutt Rottweiler. Rotty has also appeared in five video games.

The Monster Mutt trucks all look a bit different, just as the dogs they're named for look different. Rottweiler is named and designed after the rottweiler dog breed. Rottweiler the monster truck has spikes on its collar and a shorter tail than the other Monster Mutt trucks.

FUN FACT

Rottweilers are known for being strong and muscular. They also tend to be confident and brave.

TRUCK STATS

- **Year Built:** 2011
- **Body Style:** Custom 3D Dog Concept
- **Engine:** 540ci (8.8 l) Merlin

NASTY BOY

Nasty Boy started its career as part of the team known as Sturges Motorsports, which is owned by Sam Sturges. Sam's nephew Ronnie Sturges drove Nasty Boy from 1998 to 2014. A few years later, Sturges Motorsports sold the truck to Gary Ely. He's been driving Nasty Boy since 2019.

The body of Nasty Boy is a Willys truck from the 1940s made by Willys-Overland. Before the company made this model, it made jeeps used in World War II. After the war, the company debated about going back to making standard

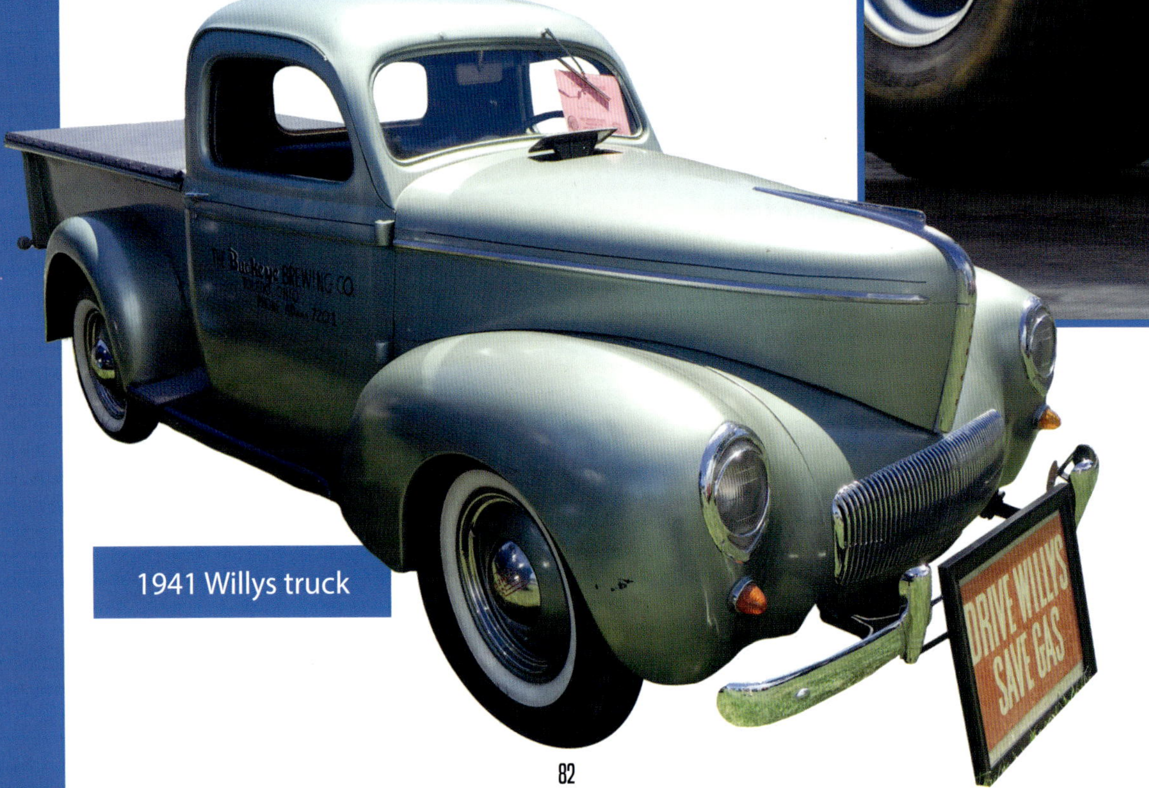

1941 Willys truck

cars. But instead, knowing customers were interested in military-style vehicles, they made the Willys truck. It was one of the only 4X4 trucks of its time. This model is still valuable to classic car collectors.

TRUCK STATS

- **Year Built**: 1996
- **Body Style**: 1940s Willys
- **Engine**: Blown Alcohol Injected 468ci (7.7 l) Chevrolet

OBSESSION

Obsession comes from California. Its driver and owner, Rick Swanson, bought it in 1996 and drove Obsession in its first competition the following year.

Swanson started racing BMX bikes when he was 10 years old. He bought an old Ford Bronco when he was in high school. And he almost immediately started building it bigger.

Obsessed is Obsession's teammate. Eric Swanson, Rick Swanson's son, is the main driver. Eric was just eight weeks old when he went to his first monster truck event. He was only 11 when he first drove a monster truck, but it wasn't until he was 18 that he began to compete.

TRUCK STATS

- **Year Built**: 1996
- **Body Style**: 2005 Ford F-350 Super Duty
- **Engine**: 540ci (8.8 l) Chevrolet Big Block

FUN FACT

To legally drive a Monster Jam truck, a driver must be at least 18 years old. They must also hold a commercial driver's license (CDL) from their local department of motor vehicles.

OVERKILL EVOLUTION

Overkill Evolution's driver is Mike Vaters II. He comes from a monster truck family. His mom, Pam Vahle, drove a monster truck called Boogey Van. And his dad, Michael Vaters Sr., runs Vaters Motorsports. He's probably best known for building and driving the truck Black Stallion.

Mike Vaters II was the first driver to win the Young Guns Shootout in his first year of driving. Before he drove monster trucks, Mike was a professional freestyle motocross driver. Mike and Overkill Evolution have competed at the Monster Jam World Finals five times.

MONSTER TRUCK TRIVIA

Higher Education is another monster truck owned by Vaters Motorsports.

TRUCK STATS

- **Year Built:** 2014
- **Body Style:** Ford F-250 Super Duty
- **Engine:** 572ci (9.4 l) Ford Supercharged Big Block
- **Awards:** Young Guns Shootout Champion, 2014; Monster Jam World Finals Freestyle Champion, 2015

TRUCK STATS

- **Year Built:** 2004
- **Body Style:** Chevrolet Silverado
- **Engine:** 540ci (8.8 l) Dart Motor

The Patriot was decorated with American symbols.

THE PATRIOT

Driver Dan Rodoni started a company called Central Coast Four-Wheel Drive in 1995. He and the company were based in California. He started working on and driving monster trucks in 2001. In 2003, he started building The Patriot, and the truck was ready for shows the next year. Having a monster truck in his hometown of Santa Cruz was a little unusual. The town isn't known for motorsports.

When it first came out, The Patriot had a silver design, with the words "Freedom Is Forever" on its sides. It was later painted blue. Different versions have included bald eagles and flags.

Before The Patriot's retirement, it ran under several other names, including Donkey Kong, Break the Chain, and El Toro Loco. In 2021, Rodoni sold The Patriot to the company Harper Motorsports. Since then, the truck has competed as both Outlaw and Outfoxed.

PURE ADRENALINE

Randy Brown built and drove Pure Adrenaline. As a kid, Brown helped build motors for his dad's trucks that were in pulling competitions. Brown started driving his dad's truck puller as soon as he had his driver's license. In 1998, Brown worked with Dan Patrick, a well-known monster truck builder. Together, they built Pure Adrenaline, which was ready for shows in 2000. Brown didn't have a CDL to drive the new monster truck. So at first, driver Gary Porter drove Pure Adrenaline.

Over the years, Brown drove quite a few trucks in addition to Pure Adrenaline. He joined the famous Grave Digger team in 2003. In 2012, Pure Adrenaline retired, and the truck was converted into a Grave Digger vehicle.

TRUCK STATS

- **Year Built**: 2000
- **Body Style**: Ford F-150; Ford F-250 Super Duty
- **Engine**: 540ci (8.8 l)

FUN FACT

A rush of adrenaline can make a person feel excited, energetic, and strong.

MONSTER TRUCK TRIVIA

The earliest versions of the truck were named Pure Adrenalin. Later versions added an "e" to the end: Pure Adrenaline.

PURE ADRENALINE
NATIONAL WILD TURKEY FEDERATION

TRUCK STATS

- **Year Built:** 2002
- **Body Style:** 2020 Dodge Ram 2500 Power Wagon
- **Engine:** 565ci (9.3 l) Supercharged Hemi
- **Awards:** MTRA Truck of the Year 2002, 2003, 2004, 2005, 2006, 2007, 2011, 2013, 2014; Monster Truck Nationals Champion 2003, 2004; Monster Truck Nationals Racing Champion 2005, 2006, 2007, 2013, 2014, 2015; Monster Truck Nationals Freestyle Champion 2005, 2013, 2014, 2015, 2016

RAMINATOR

The first version of Raminator launched in 2002. It was bright red with white-and-yellow wording and a tough-looking sheep on the sides. Around 2014, Raminator got a new black paint job. Brothers Tim Hall and Mark Hall own and drive Raminator and its teammate, Rammunition.

Raminator and driver Tim Hall used to hold the world record for fastest monster truck. They hit 99.1 miles (160 km) per hour in 2014. Other trucks have broken their record, though. As of 2022, the record holder is Joe Sylvester driving Bad Habit. They clocked 101.84 miles (164 km) per hour.

MONSTER TRUCK TRIVIA

Mark Hall and Raminator hold the world record for most monster truck national championship wins. Together, they've won 25 times.

FUN FACT

The Raminator is named after the ram, a male sheep that fights by striking with its head and horns.

RAMMUNITION

Rammunition, like its teammate Raminator, is owned by Hall Brothers Racing, based in Illinois. The two trucks are built on the same model truck with the same type of engine. In fact, the horsepower of Rammunition and Raminator are some of the most powerful in monster trucks. They debuted in the same year. Brothers Mark and

TRUCK STATS

- **Year Built**: 2002
- **Body Style**: Dodge Ram 2500 Power Wagon
- **Engine**: 565ci (9.3 l) Supercharged Hemi

FUN FACT

Hotsy, another truck on Rammunition's team, has flames along the side.

Tim Hall run the team, which also includes the trucks Hotsy and Executioner.

Geremie Dishman drove Rammunition from its debut on the racing circuit until he retired in 2010. Geremie's brother, Mat, drove the truck until 2019 when he, too, retired.

Rammunition's career was still going strong. Driver Kurt Kraehmer, who had been driving the truck's teammate Hotsy, took over. Rammunition is still touring and competing as of 2024.

104
SUBWAY SUBWAY
RAP ATTACK
Advance Auto Parts

RAP ATTACK

Dave Rappach is the owner and driver of Rap Attack. The Ohio-based driver started driving monster trucks in 1991. Seven years later, he bought Rap Attack, and he and the truck became known for epic wheelies. Rappach spends many of his weekends at monster truck shows. But when he's not monster trucking, Rappach works in construction.

Rappach says his favorite part of competing is freestyle. It can lead to surprises the fans aren't expecting. He doesn't worry much about getting hurt because trucks have so many safety features.

TRUCK STATS

- **Year Built**: 1998
- **Body Style**: GMC Sierra (1998 to 2000, 2002 to 2006), 2013 Chevy Silverado (2000 to 2002, 2006 to 2015), 2015 Chevrolet 2500 (since 2015)
- **Engine**: 572 Keith Black
- **Awards**: Monster Truck Throwdown Overall Event Champion, 2022

MONSTER TRUCK TRIVIA

Rappach once said that his biggest feat in monster trucks was having the most rollovers in the 2000 series.

FUN FACT

All monster trucks are loud, but Rap Attack is known for being one of the loudest.

RED DRAGON

If anyone has ever wanted to ride on a monster truck, Red Dragon might be their chance. This truck is based in the United Kingdom. It used to be a monster truck that competed in events. Rob Williams, who was once a European Monster Truck Champion, built it himself. The first version of Red Dragon included an air cannon on top. The truck could shoot anything that weighed less than 1,400 pounds (635 kg).

TRUCK STATS

- **Year Built**: 2010
- **Body Style**: Ford F-350 Super Duty
- **Engine**: 9.5 liter V-8

MONSTER TRUCK TRIVIA

For a few events in Europe, Red Dragon was painted with the name Energy of Freedom. The truck's bed has seats for 10 riders.

Then the truck's owners converted it. Red Dragon is still as big as a monster truck. It still has huge tires. It can drive over cars. But it is built for taking people on rides. The truck visits motorsports events, fairs, festivals, and other outdoor events in Europe. Riders must be in good health and be at least 3 feet (1 m) tall. To get in, they climb a staircase set up at the back of the truck.

SAFE AUTO
Play it Safe
MINIMIZER

SAFE AUTO MINIMIZER

This truck was initially called Safe Auto when it debuted in 2005, with the slogan "Play It Safe." Later that year, though, it was called Safe Auto Minimizer, and the logo had been dropped. During its first year, Chad Tingler drove the truck. When he moved to team Grave Digger the next year, Marc McDonald took over.

McDonald was a rookie, but he drove well enough to be invited to the World Finals. He and Safe Auto Minimizer would compete at the Monster Truck World Finals four years in a row. In 2008, the truck's sponsor company updated its logo. So the truck got a new design too.

McDonald and Safe Auto Minimizer competed until 2009, when its sponsor company ended its contract with Monster Jam. McDonald started driving the truck El Toro Loco instead.

TRUCK STATS

- **Year Built**: 2005
- **Body Style**: Ford F-150
- **Engine**: 540ci (8.8 l) Merlin

MONSTER TRUCK TRIVIA

Safe Auto Minimizer's name comes from the company that sponsors it—an insurance company called Safe Auto.

SAMSON

The first version of Samson, built in 1983, was bright red with blue-and-yellow print. Five years later, owner and driver Don Maples sold Samson to driver Dan Patrick.

In the 1990s, Samson appeared in a few different monster truck shows. Patrick also arranged a contract with a TV show called *American Gladiators*. In the show, everyday people competed against bodybuilders in athletic events. To help advertise the show at monster truck events, Samson got a new look in 1993. It was painted red, white, and blue. But the biggest change to its look was its new muscular arms. They reach from the cab to the hood, ending in strong punching fists. Samson and Patrick started competing at Monster Jam several years later, in 1997.

Patrick retired from driving in 2013. He was inducted into the International Monster Truck Hall of Fame the same year. But Samson

TRUCK STATS

- **Year Built**: 1983
- **Body Style**: Custom 2006 Chevrolet Silverado Concept
- **Engine**: 565ci (9.3 l) Brad Anderson Hemi

FUN FACT

Samson was named after a character from the Bible who was known for his extraordinary strength.

didn't retire. Patrick's daughter, Allison Patrick, started driving
the truck. Sometimes, Allison's husband,
Rick Steffens, drives Samson. When
Allison isn't driving Samson,
she works as a nurse.

Scooby-Doo!

SCOOBY-DOO

You might know Scooby-Doo's character from the cartoon about a group of kids who solve mysteries. This version is a little tougher, but it still has a floppy tail and brown ears.

Driver Linsey Read has been a fan of monster trucks since she was a kid. As an adult, Read had a chance to drive a different kind of truck at a Monster Jam event. She did so well that people told her she should try driving monster trucks! After training at Monster Jam University, she got her job driving Scooby-Doo.

Scooby-Doo has competed at the Monster Jam World Finals every year since its debut. In 2014, driver Nicole Johnson and the truck landed its first backflip!

MONSTER TRUCK TRIVIA

Scooby-Doo's theme song on the track is "Scooby-Doo, Where Are You?" by MxPx.

FUN FACT

Scooby-Doo (the cartoon and the truck) is a type of dog called a Great Dane.

SHATTERED

When Shattered debuted in 2004, its color scheme was blue and yellow. A design of cracks ran along the yellow portions. Over the years, the truck's colors changed slightly— sometimes orange instead

TRUCK STATS

- **Year Built**: 2004
- **Body Style**: Chevrolet Extended Cab S-10 (2004 to 2005, 2008), Jeep Scrambler (2006 to 2007), 2002 Ford F-150 (2009)
- **Engine**: 540ci (8.8 l) Merlin

FUN FACT

In 2009, Shattered was sold. Its name changed to Raptor's Revenge.

of yellow, purple instead of blue. It also used different body styles, including a Chevrolet S-10, a Ford F-150, and a Jeep Scrambler.

Scott Anderson, who lives in Idaho, owned and drove Shattered. He worked with stock car racing before he fell in love with monster trucks. Over the years, Anderson owned at least seven different monster trucks.

In keeping with its shifting identity, Shattered sometimes went by different names. Other names on the truck included Blue Lightning and Kaptain Insano 2.

SHATTERED
RD TRU

SHREDDER

Mark Pedersen started driving Shredder in 2012. Pederson is also the owner of Reptoid Racing, home of the bright green reptile-like monster truck known as Reptoid. Before Shredder became known as Shredder, it was already a monster truck. It was named Samson 1 Tribute. It was a tribute, or acknowledgment, to the monster truck Samson.

By 2015, Shredder had been converted to a ride truck. Six riders can sit on top of Shredder, while a driver in the cab takes them on a monster truck adventure. To get to their seats, guests climb up a moveable staircase set up behind the truck. Shredder the ride truck and the monster truck Reptoid are still managed by Reptoid Racing. They visit county fairs, fundraising events, local truck shows, and more.

TRUCK STATS

- **Year Built**: 2012
- **Body Style**: 1987 Chevrolet
- **Engine**: 540ci (8.8 l) Merlin
- **Awards**: 2015 Best in Show, Bluegill Frolic in Marcellus, Michigan

FUN FACT

A version of Shredder that looks just like the original is still around. It was displayed at the 2023 Detroit Autorama, a specialty car show in Michigan.

Driven By Alan Vaughan
Slingshot
CHROME
slingshot2014
Find us on
facebook.
Y1I2 ERB
T244 KKJ
NLB

SLINGSHOT

Karl Swallow and his family started building Slingshot in England in 2003. At first, it used a gas engine (called petrol in its home country). Most monster trucks use a type of fuel called methanol, not gas. The following year, Swallow and Slingshot started racing. They came in third place at the 2005 European Monster Truck Racing Championship. The gas-fueled engine didn't last long. Swallow wanted his truck to have an engine more like the trucks he was competing against. Those were mostly methanol engines. Swallow upgraded Slingshot's engine in 2006.

Karl Swallow died in 2012, and his nephew, Alan Vaughn, took over driving Slingshot. These days, there are three Slingshots. They mostly work in the United Kingdom. One is a standard monster truck. It competes in monster truck races and other events. The other two are ride trucks. They visit fairs, festivals, and other outdoor events.

TRUCK STATS

- **Year Built**: 2004
- **Body Style**: 2004 Chevrolet Silverado
- **Engine**: Supercharged 528ci (8.7 l) Big Block Chevy

FUN FACT

Slingshot was the first monster truck from Europe to jump over a bus.

SPIDER-MAN

Spider-Man has had three different parts to its career, with pauses in between. The first Spider-Man contract between Marvel Comics and Feld Entertainment ran from 2001 to 2003. That truck was built on the 1963 Cheetah, a race car that originally included a 327ci (5.6 l) Corvette engine. During this phase, Spider-Man appeared in the video game *Monster Jam: Maximum Destruction*.

Marvel's next Spider-Man contract started in 2010, along with Iron Man. Before the contract expired in 2014, Spider-Man would compete in several Monster Jam World Finals, as well as heading overseas to Spain, Costa Rica, and Panama.

The third monster truck contract between Marvel and Feld Entertainment kicked off in 2023. It included a new Spider-Man, along with Iron Man, Thor, and Black Panther.

FUN FACT

The 2023 redesigned Spider-Man includes a net gun, so it can shoot webs.

TRUCK STATS

- **Year Built**: 2001
- **Body Style**: 1963 Cheetah; Custom 3D Spider-Man Concept
- **Engine**: 540ci (8.8 l) Merlin
- **Awards**: Young Guns Shootout Champion 2012

Spider-Man, 2011

STONE CRUSHER

Stone Crusher crushes more than stone! This truck started its career in 2005, when owner Steve Sims bought a retired Monster Jam truck called Backdraft. Sims reworked and repainted the truck, turning it into Stone Crusher. Stone Crusher is decorated with flames, cracked rock, and wild-looking cave people.

Steve Sims and Stone Crusher made it to the Monster Jam World Finals eight years in a row.

Sims's day job is managing a stone and granite company. One day, long before Stone Crusher, the owner and driver of Grave Digger, Dennis Anderson, asked Sims to make him some countertops. Sims agreed, but he asked for payment other than money. He wanted Anderson to bring Grave Digger to his child's birthday party. Anderson agreed, and a business relationship soon formed. The two have been connected through monster trucks ever since.

TRUCK STATS

- **Year Built**: 2005
- **Body Style**: Ford F-250; Ford F-350
- **Engine**: 572ci (9.4 l) Ford Performance
- **Awards**: Monster Jam Team of the Year, 2008, 2009, and 2011

MONSTER TRUCK TRIVIA

Monster trucks have become very popular at birthday parties. Steve Sims was able to have a real monster truck at his child's birthday party. But inflatable monster truck bounce houses are much more common.

SWAMP THING

Swamp Thing is an English monster truck. It tours in Europe and the United Kingdom. Sometimes, it also competes at Monster Jam in the United States. Swamp Thing's owner and driver is Tony Dixon. When Dixon was very young, he used to watch monster trucks on television. He decided that someday he would own a monster truck himself.

TRUCK STATS

- **Year Built**: 2003
- **Body Style**: Ford F-350 Super Duty
- **Engine**: 572ci (9.4 l) Tall Block, BDS Supercharger
- **Awards**: 2016 UK Monster Truck Nationals Racing Winner; European Monster Truck Racing Champion 2003 to 2007

MONSTER TRUCK TRIVIA

Swamp Thing has appeared in two British TV shows. In 2007, it was part of *ScrapHeap Challenge*. The show *Top Gear* showed off Swamp Thing in 2008.

In 2003, Dixon was ready to debut Swamp Thing, with its green alligator design and sharp white teeth across the front. Dixon and Swamp Thing have been driving in shows and competitions ever since. Dixon's YouTube channel shows highlights from monster truck events, as well as project building in his workshop. Dixon's wife and two kids also work on the Swamp Thing team. The family lives in a town called Melksham in southwest England.

THOR

Thor is a Swedish monster truck owned by a company called Viking Monster Trucks. Its owner and driver, Lars Larsson, built it from parts of a truck formerly known as Blown Thunder. Over the years, Thor has raced at European Monster Jam and other local events. In addition to Larsson, Patrik Tenbrock, Anders Flogard, and Peter Nyman have driven Thor.

Thor the monster truck is named for the character Thor in Norse mythology. Norse refers to Norwegian or Scandinavian people and culture. In these myths, Thor was a god of lightning and thunder. He was known for being strong, smart, and able to control the weather. He had a magical hammer that could destroy almost anything, including enemies. These are all powerful qualities in a god . . . or a monster truck.

There is also an American monster truck named Thor. The American Thor has visited Europe a few times. But it has no connection to the Swedish monster truck Thor.

Tiger Shark crushes cars during a Hot Wheels Monster Trucks Live event.

TIGER SHARK

Tiger Shark started out as a Hot Wheels toy design in 2018. It has orange-and-black stripes, like a tiger. It also has fins, like a shark. The next year, Tiger Shark was built into an actual monster truck. It joined the competition at the Hot Wheels Monster Trucks Live show. In each event of this show, eight trucks competed. Versions of Tiger Shark have traveled in Europe and Canada, as well as in the United States.

Tiger Shark is part of a racing team called Team Beast. The Dayton, Ohio, shop that manages the team is Holman Motorsports. Driver and owner Bobby Holman owns Tiger Shark. In 2021, Bobby Holman joined the International Monster Truck Hall of Fame. Most of Tiger Shark's events are Hot Wheels monster truck shows.

TRUCK STATS

- **Year Built**: 2019
- **Body Style**: PEI/Custom-built Shark
- **Engine**: 540ci (8.8 l) Chevrolet

FUN FACT

The Hot Wheels 2019 monster truck tour also had a TV show. It was called *Hot Wheels Monster Trucks Live: Crushing It!*

TOXIC

Toxic got its start in 2010 with Petri Motorsports in New York. Brothers Travis and Larry Petri managed and drove the truck at events on the east coasts of the United States and Canada. Between 2015 and 2018, Kris Gilbert of Gilbert Motorsports owned Toxic. Cory Snyder started driving the truck that year too. In 2018, Cory Snyder and his dad Jay Snyder bought Toxic. Their company, Warped Motor Sports, had been managing and driving monster trucks for 20 years by that point.

In 2020, the Snyders built a new version of the truck, calling it Toxic 2.0. The new version was created with a chassis from Dan Patrick's company Patrick Enterprises. The "Patrick chassis" is made to monster truck specifications and doesn't need extra work from the builder. Another word used to describe them is "turn-key." That means the buyer can just turn the key and go. It's different from most monster trucks, which need a lot of mechanical know-how from their builders.

TRUCK STATS

- **Year Built**: 2010
- **Body Style**: Ford F-250 Super Duty
- **Engine**: 540ci (8.8 l) BBC (Toxic 1.0); 557ci (9.1 l) BBC (Toxic 2.0)

MONSTER TRUCK TRIVIA

Monster truck drivers keep fire extinguishers in their truck cabs, but fires are rare. However, in 2007, Air Force Afterburner caught fire twice in two months. Both fires began after the truck crashed.

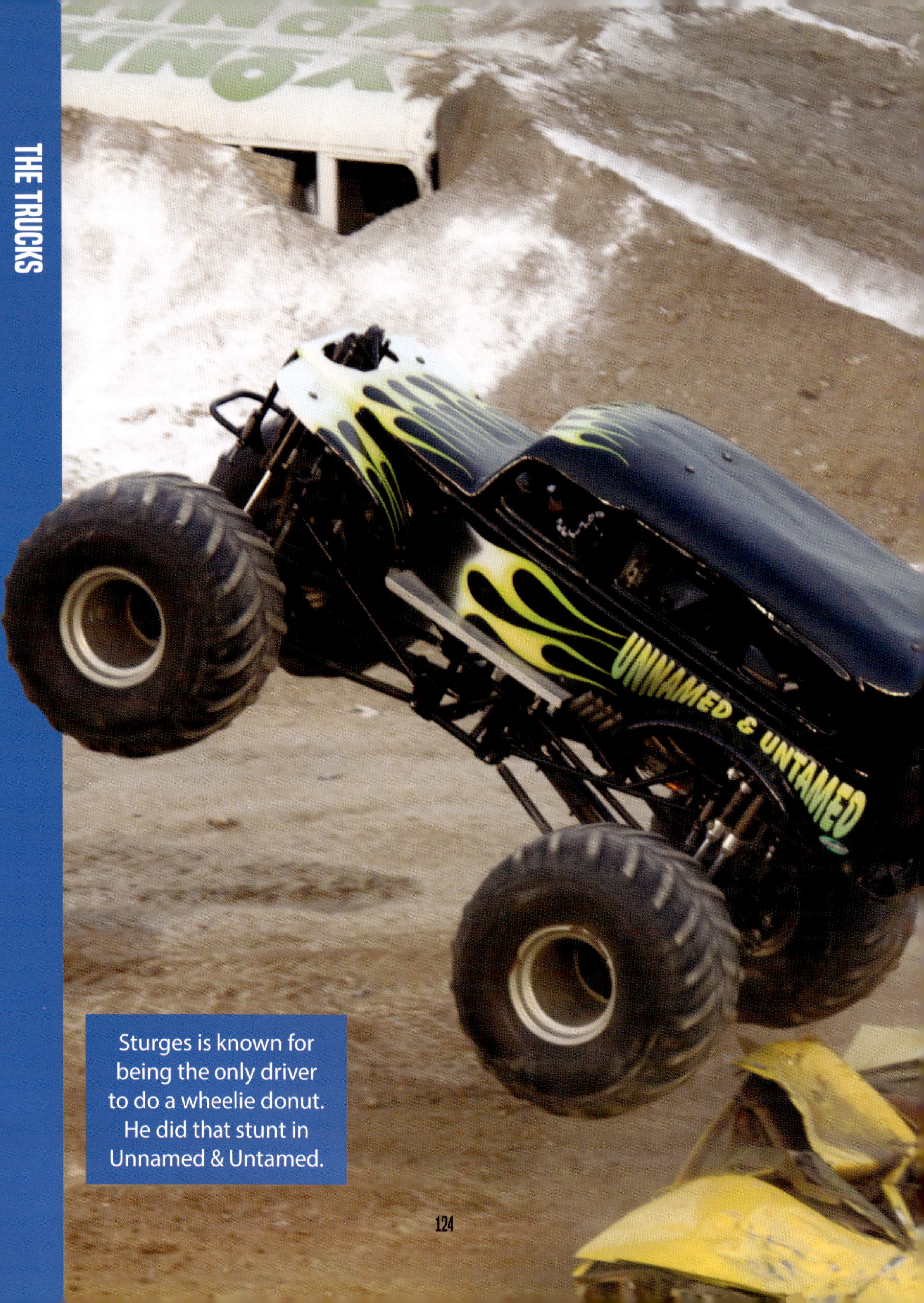

Sturges is known for being the only driver to do a wheelie donut. He did that stunt in Unnamed & Untamed.

UNNAMED & UNTAMED

Unnamed & Untamed started its racing life as a mud truck in the 1980s. The first version of the truck was built from an old military ambulance. After a few years of mud racing, its owners started turning it into a monster truck. The first monster truck version of Unnamed & Untamed was pink and teal. Two years later, its paint job would be yellow. Over its career, Unnamed & Untamed also had a splatter design, as well as a black one with green flames.

Sam Sturges, owner of Sturges Motorsports, bought Unnamed & Untamed in 1996. His company also owned the truck Nasty Boy. Sturges retired from monster truck driving in 2019. He sold both trucks. He still builds jet trucks, which are trucks made with jet engines.

TRUCK STATS

- **Year Built**: 1990
- **Body Style**: 1942 Dodge Carryall
- **Engine**: Blown Alcohol Injected 468ci (7.7 l) Chevrolet

FUN FACT

One of Sturges's early monster trucks was made from a bright yellow school bus. Its name was Kool Bus.

ZOMBIE

In 2012, Monster Jam wanted to create a new truck. And this time, they wanted to know what fans wanted in a truck. So fans voted on a few choices for possible new trucks. The winner was Zombie, perhaps the creepiest monster truck of all time. Zombie made its debut in 2013, looking like a bloody, decaying zombie. This truck has rotting teeth and free-floating arms that stick out like a zombie's. Sean Duhan, Zombie's first driver, used to dress up in zombie makeup to drive the truck.

Fans in the stadium like to stick out their hands like zombies when Zombie is competing. It almost looks like a zombie dance. During monster truck events, sometimes hands or other body parts fly off of Zombie.

TRUCK STATS

- **Year Built**: 2013
- **Body Style**: Custom Ford F-150 Zombie Concept
- **Engine**: 540ci (8.8 l) Merlin
- **Awards**: Two World Records in 2020: Most Donuts in a Monster Truck in One Minute and Most Consecutive Donuts in a Monster Truck

126

FUN FACT

Fan favorite Zombie has been to every Monster Jam World Finals since its start.

MONSTER JAM

Monster Jam is one of the best-known monster truck events. It's owned by a company called Feld Motorsports, based in Florida. The parent company of Feld Motorsports is Feld Entertainment, which owns other big shows, including Disney on Ice, Ringling Bros., and Barnum & Bailey. Monster Jam hosts about 400 events in the United States each year, as well as some in other countries. The company sells more than 4 million tickets per year.

Fans can meet the drivers and crew at the Monster Jam pit party, which happens before the main event. Fans can get close up to the trucks and see how tall those wheels really are! Sometimes, pit parties include remote-controlled truck races or monster truck craft projects.

MONSTER TRUCK TRIVIA

Hot Wheels has a traveling monster truck show too. Their events tend to include fewer trucks and safer tricks than Monster Jam. While all monster truck events are family friendly, Hot Wheels is especially geared for kids.

Disney XD
El Toro Loco
MONSTER

Max-D performs during a
Monster Jam event.

MONSTER JAM WORLD FINALS

The Monster Jam World Finals happen once a year. In 2023, more than 50,000 fans came to the show. During this exciting two-day event, about 24 trucks are invited to compete. On the first day, the trucks compete in races. The race course often includes ramp jumps.

Overnight, the track crews take down the course and then rebuild a new one, making it different for the next day. On the second day, the trucks get a little wilder in the freestyle competition. Each truck gets two minutes to do its best. The audience rates the freestyle event, giving each truck a score between 1 and 10.

MONSTER TRUCK TRIVIA

Most people credit Dennis Anderson with the idea of the freestyle event. He suggested that the trucks should have an encore, or small extra show after the main one. Over time, drivers showed off different moves, and this became what is now the freestyle.

A muddy course makes challenging stunts more difficult to perform.

THE COMPETITION

In a standard Monster Jam competition, each truck does two main events. The first one is a race on a dirt track, usually with a jump ramp along the way. This one is all about speed. All competing trucks are set up in a competition bracket, two trucks per race. Winners move to the next round and compete again.

After that is freestyle. A truck is given a limited time to do whatever the driver wants. This includes jumps and stunts. There aren't many rules. Even if a driver has a plan, sometimes things change. The truck doesn't always move as expected. A driver can try to do the same jump twice, but it may not land the same way. In freestyle, each truck and driver receive scores from 1 to 10 from each judge. Then the scores are averaged. At Monster Jam, the audience judges the freestyle portion, and their scores decide the winner.

MONSTER TRUCK TRIVIA

Monster Jam usually has special events in addition to the main two. These might be trucks doing donuts or wheelies. Or other vehicles, such as four-wheelers or dirt bikes, might try obstacle courses on the track.

Big Bash League jumps over cars at a Monster Jam in Australia.

Allianz Parque
Allianz Seguros
MONSTER JAM
BKT

STADIUMS AND TRACKS

At a Monster Jam show, the front rows of the stadium closest to the trucks are blocked off for safety. Sometimes, pieces and parts fly off trucks. In a crash, a truck or its engine could catch fire. Having that space between the trucks and the audience keeps fans safe.

Most arenas or other event spaces host lots of events, not just monster trucks. Some arenas host other sporting events, like football games. Some host large music concerts. So for every monster truck event, a new track or course is built.

Different monster truck events need different tracks. The workers who build the tracks use equipment such as excavators, which have shovels at the end of a moveable arm. They also use loaders, which have scooping plow pieces, to shape the dirt into tracks. The track needs ramps for jumps and other stunts. Some ramps are 10 feet (3 m) tall. During many shows, there's a break to smooth the dirt and take away broken truck pieces.

BRINGING IN THE DIRT

Believe it or not, there are different kinds of dirt. But anyone who builds monster truck tracks knows this fact. The traits of the dirt used in an arena can affect how the trucks drive. The dirt on the floor at a monster truck show is usually a mix of sand and clay, with more clay than sand. That makes it easy to shape. The trucks don't get stuck, and they don't smash through the dirt to the floor below it.

Monster truck shows have workers whose job is to put this dirt in place. Monster Jam even has its own dirt for each stadium it uses. The company's dirt manager arranges for the dirt to be stored nearby. Then, when it's time for an event, dump trucks fill up with loads of dirt and pour it in the arena. Over a couple of days, up to 600 truckloads of dirt might be moved. When the Monster Jam event is over, the trucks take the dirt back to its storage location.

FUN FACT

In Tampa, Florida, Monster Jam stores its dirt in a big hole in the parking lot. Guests at the stadium park their cars on top.

The dirt on monster truck tracks is generally at least 8 to 10 inches (20 to 25 cm) deep. Underneath that is usually a layer of plywood and a layer of plastic covering the whole arena.

OTHER EVENTS AND SERIES

Monster Jam might be the best-known monster truck show, but it isn't the only one. Hot Wheels Monster Trucks Live has what it calls a glow party, where the stadium is dark and the trucks have glowing lights during their runs.

WGAS Motorsports organizes shows in the western part of the United States, often at state and county fairs. The group has been in business for more than 30 years. It started with tractor

pulling and mud racing. In addition to monster truck competitions, the company's events include motocross, demolition derbies, and more.

Monster Truckz travels throughout the eastern part of the United States. They put on action-packed shows starring their own monster trucks and dirt bike stunts. Many of the shows offer guest rides on a monster truck too.

The United Kingdom has its own set of monster truck shows. Truckfest has been around since 1983 and holds eight events per year around the country. All kinds of trucks show off at Truckfest, including monster trucks. About 250,000 people visit Truckfest every year.

MONSTER TRUCK TRIVIA

The earliest freestyle events were mostly about crushing cars. Back in 1989, driver Mike Welch liked to smash cars, roll his truck over, and then do more tricks.

Truckfest features all kinds of trucks, such as this Leyland Landtrain wheelie truck.

THE PLANNERS AND ORGANIZERS

A monster truck event starts long before anyone arrives at the arena. People who coordinate the shows must book arenas and plan schedules. They also reserve flights and hotels for the drivers and crew.

Organizers also plan what the event tracks will look like. They use computer programs and toy monster trucks to help them imagine the tracks.

Once an event or tour begins, teams of people make sure everything is where it needs to be, and they get it there on time. They make sure everyone has what they need to put on a great show.

The chaos of so many moving people, parts, and trucks is tightly controlled. The organizing team has a master plan on who moves where and when. They know about how long each event will take. They know

Most of the trucks owned by Monster Jam are kept in a huge warehouse in Florida when they are not on location at an event.

Mini monster trucks are moved onto the track for fans to race.

who's competing first, last, and in between. They must be good at their jobs so that the event runs seamlessly. If a show runs smoothly, the audience doesn't even realize anything is happening behind the scenes.

Monster truck fans view the track and trucks before a Monster Jam in the Philippines.

TRUCK CREWS

Monster truck mechanics are able to replace parts and repair anything that breaks. Monster trucks are driven hard. They bounce around. They turn upside-down. They land on their sides. Parts on a monster truck break often. Most trucks have their own mechanics or team of mechanics that travel with them. Monster Jam has its own mechanics, who work on any or all of the Monster Jam trucks.

A monster truck event has two areas called pits—a hot pit and a cold pit. The busiest place at a monster truck event might be the hot pit. That's where trucks wait their turn to race. It's where trucks go when they leave the arena after their events. The only people allowed in the hot pit are drivers and crews.

In the cold pit, crews work on anything that breaks during those exciting tricks and turns. During a two-day event, crews are likely to work on trucks all night. They're fixing anything that broke on the first day, to get it ready for the second day. A well-organized pile of mechanical parts includes tires, wheels, and motors. There may also be piles of truck body parts, such as fins or spikes.

FUN FACT

It takes about two hours to replace a broken truck motor. But it only takes a few minutes to replace a monster truck tire.

A mechanic fills the tires on the monster truck Anger Management.

ON THE ROAD

Monster trucks aren't allowed to drive on regular streets or highways. To get to their events, the trucks first have to be prepped. Their 66-inch (168 cm) tires come off, and smaller tires are put on. Then the trucks roll on their small travel tires, right into a huge semitrailer built especially for monster trucks. If trucks are going overseas, they ride in large metal containers on cargo ships.

FUN FACT

One monster truck safety rule says that drivers must be able to turn off their truck's engine with their eyes closed.

Camden Murphy with his monster truck Dragonoid

V8 Bomber at Hot Wheels
Monster Trucks Live in 2021

The trailers that transport monster trucks are like travel auto shops. They have the tools and equipment the truck's mechanic needs to make repairs.

MONSTER TRUCK TRIVIA

The floor of a monster truck cab, where the driver sits, is either completely open or made of clear plastic. That allows the driver to see the ground underneath.

MONSTER TRUCK RACING ASSOCIATION

The group that sets rules for monster trucks is called the Monster Truck Racing Association (MTRA). In the 1980s, the sport was becoming popular. More people wanted to build and drive monster trucks. With so many huge trucks and engines around, Bob Chandler and George Carpenter set up a meeting with other drivers. They wanted to make sure that monster truck events were safe for drivers, crews, and audiences.

In 1987, 49 truck drivers and owners held MTRA's first official meeting. Together, they created a board of directors and a set of standard safety rules for trucks and events. They also set up membership levels and costs to become a member of MTRA. The group still oversees monster trucks in the United States. Most monster truck teams and companies follow MTRA's official rule book.

MONSTER TRUCK TRIVIA

One rule MTRA created early on was that all trucks needed to be inspected for safety. If an MTRA member wanted to become an inspector, they had to take a four-hour training course.

Driver Nick Pagliarulo works on his monster truck Kraken.

DENNIS ANDERSON

When Dennis Anderson was growing up, he planned to become a farmer. He lived near the border between Virginia and North Carolina. One of his favorite hobbies was mud bogging. That means that people replaced the tires on their pickup trucks with tractor tires. And then they went off-roading through the mud. In 1982, Anderson started adding tractor parts to an old 1952 Ford pickup.

When someone teased him about building a truck from junk, Anderson said he'd build him a grave out of that junk. The truck became known as Grave Digger. Anderson started a workshop where he fixed other people's cars as well as his own. Over the years, the team has grown and so has the number of Grave Digger trucks. His shop, Digger's Dungeon, grew into a tourist attraction with a diner, a shop, and old monster trucks on display.

Anderson became one of the biggest names in monster truck history. He was inducted into the International Monster Truck Hall of Fame in 2012. He has been a Monster Jam World Finals champion four times.

> **FUN FACT**
>
> Anderson's daughter, Krysten, and his three sons, Ryan, Adam, and Weston, also drive monster trucks.

MONSTER TRUCK TRIVIA

Anderson's shop, Digger's Dungeon, has become a landmark for monster truck fans. Visitors can see a Grave Digger truck. They can also take a ride on a real monster truck.

GEORGE BALHAN

George Balhan is best known for driving the trucks An Escalade and Mohawk Warrior. He drove monster trucks from 2003 to 2017, and he specialized in wheelies and donuts. Sometimes, in the middle of performing a donut, Balhan removed the steering wheel from his truck and held it out through the opening of the roof.

Balhan holds the world record for the most backflips in a row during a competition. He and Mohawk Warrior did two during a 2012 Monster Jam freestyle event. Balhan was so popular with fans that a toy action figure of him was made, complete with a mohawk and a Mohawk Warrior jacket.

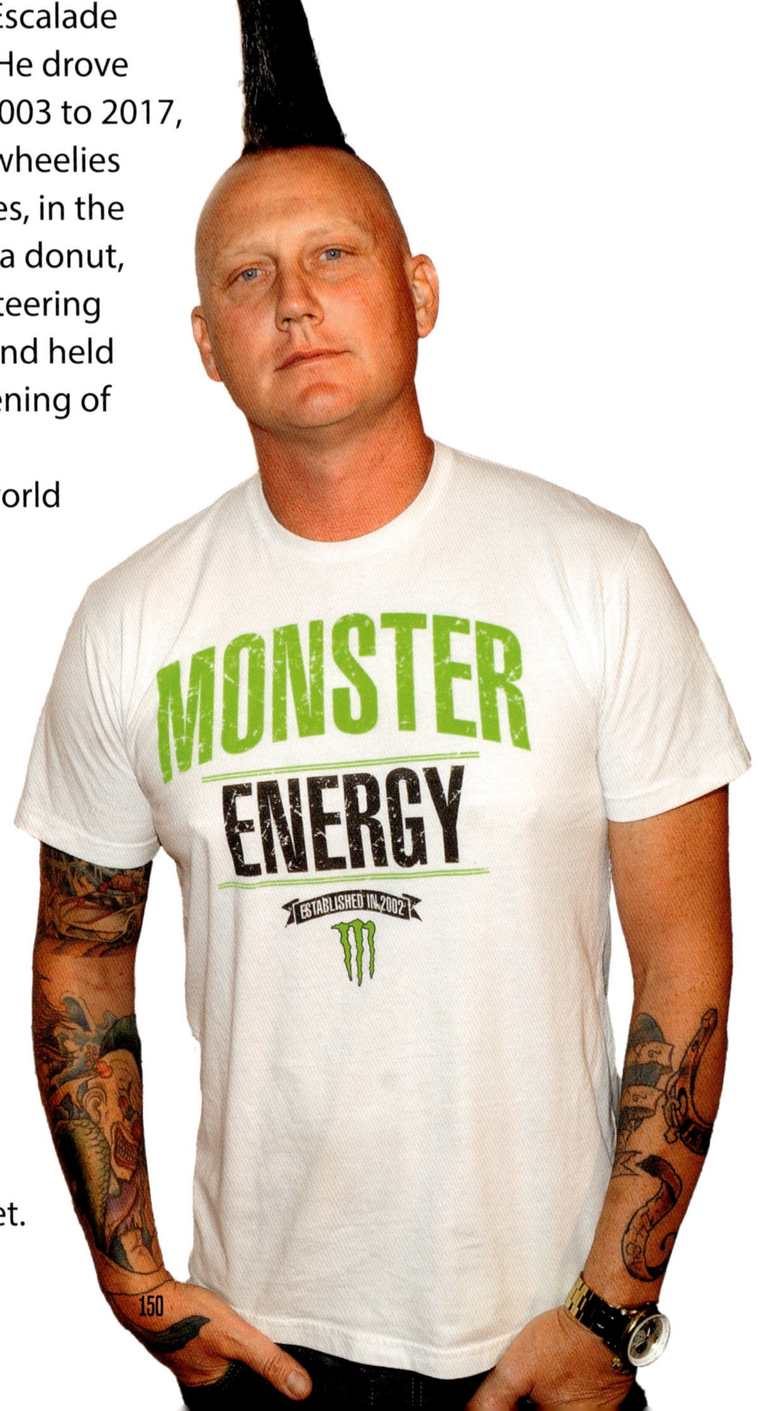

CHARLES BENNS

Charles Benns drove monster trucks from 2004 to 2013. He drove a truck called Pitbull between 2004 and 2010. He also spent a few years driving Monster Mutt Rottweiler. Benns grew his hair long so he could donate it to groups that make wigs for sick kids who've lost their hair. He also gave money to a children's hospital in his hometown in New Mexico. Benns received the Monster Jam Humanitarian of the Year award multiple times.

BOB CHANDLER

In the 1970s, Bob Chandler was a construction worker and a carpenter. He lived near St. Louis, Missouri, with his wife, Marilyn. They liked to camp. They drove their Ford pickup out along a river, as far as they could go. At the time, Bob didn't know anyone else who liked to go off-road driving. Bob liked to tinker with the truck. He added bigger, stronger parts for off-roading. It was hard to find parts, so the Chandlers started a shop.

Chandler was still driving his truck in places with no roads. And when he did, something usually broke. His driving earned him a nickname. Because Chandler couldn't keep his foot off

the gas pedal, his employees called him Bigfoot. And soon, that was the truck's name too. These days, people call him the inventor of the monster truck.

With each version of Bigfoot, Chandler kept making improvements. He designed new parts and used new materials. His changes made monster trucks safer and stronger. His truck shop is still in business too. Fifty years later, Chandler's invention is loved around the world.

FUN FACT

Chandler was one of the founding members of the MTRA, which makes safety rules that apply to all monster trucks.

CYNTHIA GAUTHIER

When Canadian driver Cynthia Gauthier was a kid, she and her mechanic dad watched snowmobiling and dirt bike races as well as NASCAR events. Gauthier started racing dirt bikes in motocross when she was 18 years old. A few years later, she met some people in Monster Jam and started working on the crews.

In 2015, Gauthier began driving monster trucks. She is best known for driving Monster Mutt Dalmatian. Recently, she has also driven Lucas Stabilizer. She loves backflips and getting lots of air, or going really high in a jump. In 2019, she won the Monster Jam High Jump World Championship, with a jump of 45.472 feet (14 m).

Cynthia Gauthier has an accounting degree and a welding certificate.

BECKY MCDONOUGH

Becky McDonough started her monster truck career as a mechanic. She studied high-performance engines and chassis fabrication in college.

Then she landed a job as a mechanic for Monster Jam. Starting around 2006, she became crew chief for the truck Nitro Circus. Her dream, though, was to drive the trucks. In 2010, she drove Donkey Kong, but in 2012, she moved to El Toro Loco. Becky has driven other trucks since then, but she mostly drives El Toro Loco.

FUN FACT

Becky McDonough owns a company that makes clothing for women who love motorsports.

156

MADUSA, A.K.A. DEBRA MICELI

Debra Miceli drives under the name Madusa. In high school, she was a gymnast who loved dirt bikes and ATVs. Before she started driving monster trucks, she was a professional wrestler. Miceli was the women's WWE champion three times before moving to the WWC.

In 1999, the USHRA asked Miceli if she'd like to try driving monster trucks. She had the chance to train with Dennis Anderson, driver of the famous Grave Digger, in his backyard. In 2000, she along with the truck Madusa started making a name for themselves in monster trucks.

Her nickname in the monster truck world is the "Queen of Carnage." Miceli and Madusa won the 2004 Monster Truck World Finals. They beat Dennis Anderson and Grave Digger.

Madusa is often called the first woman in monster trucks. But there were others before her. One early driver was Pam Vahle. In 1993, she built and drove a truck called Boogey Van. She sold the truck in 1999, but she continued to drive it until 2001. She is the mother of driver Mikey Vaters II.

FUN FACT

In 2019, driver Linsey Read became the second female driver to win the Monster Truck World Finals, in Scooby-Doo.

TOM MEENTS

Tom Meents is a big name in the monster truck world. He has won 14 Monster Jam World Finals championships. Six of these were for racing, and six were for freestyle. The other two were for the two-wheel skills challenge, which are tricks on two wheels. Meents is also the founder of Monster Jam University, which trains new Monster Jam drivers.

Meents started thinking about driving monster trucks when he was just 10 years old. When he was a little older, he worked as a mechanic for a Ford dealership. Most monster truck drivers know more than just driving. They need to be able to repair trucks, too, since their wild driving can result in so many crashes.

Before he drove and worked on monster trucks, Meents was a mud racing driver. His mud racing truck was called Shake Me.

Tom Meents before attempting to set a Guinness World Record as the first to land a front flip in competition.

His leap into monster trucks came in 1993, when he drove a truck called Monster Patrol. He drove a few other trucks over the years before focusing on Maximum Destruction, which was later shortened to Max-D, in 2003. In 2015, Meents and Max-D made the first attempt at a front flip in a competition. But they didn't quite make it—the front tires didn't land on the ground.

His biggest rival in the monster truck arena is Dennis Anderson, driver of Grave Digger. It's a friendly rivalry. Meents once drove Grave Digger when Anderson was hurt and couldn't drive.

BARI MUSAWWIR

Bari Musawwir holds quite a few records and titles. He went to his first monster truck show when he was six years old. Even then, he knew he wanted to drive monster trucks. A few years later, he started competing in remote-controlled car competitions. He started running radio-controlled truck events at Monster Jam pit parties. That's where he met monster truck owner and driver Scott Hartsock.

Hard work and good connections happened, and eventually Musawwir had the chance to drive a monster truck. He was Monster Jam's rookie of the year in 2011. Over the years, he's driven trucks including Backwards Bob, El Toro Loco, Spider-Man, and Zombie.

MONSTER TRUCK TRIVIA

In 2013, Bari Musawwir, driving Spider-Man, made history at the Monster Jam World Finals. He was the first Black driver to compete at the World Finals.

CHARLIE PAUKEN

Charlie Pauken has been driving monster trucks since 1987. In his first truck, Excaliber, he won the Thunder Nationals three times. Beginning in 1999, Pauken joined the Grave Digger team. He stayed with them until 2021. But he has driven other trucks as well, including Bulldozer and Megalodon. He and Monster Mutt won a Monster Jam World Finals freestyle championship in 2010.

MONSTER JAM UNIVERSITY

How do all those monster truck drivers learn to drive? Do they just take the same driver's education class as everyone else? Driving a 10,000-pound (4,536 kg) monster truck is much different from driving a regular car. That's where Monster Jam University comes in. Anyone who wants to drive for Monster Jam must complete this training.

The head instructor and founder of Monster Jam University is driver Tom Meents. He's won 14 world championships, among other successes. Most student drivers call him the Professor. Meents built a training course on his own property in rural Illinois. It became the official Monster Jam driver training.

To get into most monster trucks, a driver goes under the body and climbs up through the frame.

Some Monster Jam University students learn the mechanic side of monster trucks.

MJU holds tryouts once a year, and those tryouts last about three days. Anyone can apply. First, drivers in training practice getting into a truck and learning how the truck works. Then, for a full day, they learn about safety. The last stage, which lasts at least nine days, is hands-on training in a truck. Students practice driving laps and jumping ramps. Mostly, they learn to handle the truck. That includes watching videos of themselves driving to learn what they could do better.

FUN FACT

Monster Jam University is part of the University of Northwestern Ohio. Students there are known as the Racers.

RAMP JUMP

Racing is part of the excitement of a monster truck competition. But many fans come for the stunts and tricks of the freestyle event. Those include jumping over cars, flipping upside down in the air, traveling with only two of four wheels on the ground, and spinning in circles. Drivers say that they might do the same steps for a trick every time, but the truck doesn't always land the same. Monster truck stunts can even surprise their drivers.

The first stunt most drivers learn is a jump. To do this, the driver starts a few truck lengths from a ramp. Then they put the gas pedal to the floor until the truck drives up and off the ramp into the air. Some jumps are higher than others.

Landing a monster truck can be as tricky as launching it. Drivers keep the wheels straight. They try to land on all four tires. Then, just as they hit the ground, they hit the gas hard. That can turn a bad landing into a good one.

MONSTER TRUCK TRIVIA

The world record jump height is 33 feet, 9.6 inches (10 m). Krysten Anderson set that record in Grave Digger in 2020.

GRAVE DIGGER
GRAVE D
111
113
BKT
BKT
BKT
MONSTER JAM
MONSTER JAM
Great Clips
Great Clips
MonsterJam.co

Tom Meents's 2015 unsuccessful attempt to land the first-ever front flip of a monster truck.

FLIPS

In a front flip, the monster truck jumps off the ground and rolls forward in a circle, like a somersault or front roll in gymnastics. A backflip is similar, but the truck is circling backward through the air. A key part of the flip is landing. If the truck doesn't land on its wheels, the flip isn't complete.

The first driver to land a backflip in competition was Cam McQueen. He was competing at Jacksonville Monster Jam in 2010. The first driver to land a backflip outside of competition was Tom Meents. He and Maximum Destruction landed a double backflip in 2015.

Drivers used to have an extra option on flips. It was called the corkscrew. When a truck goes up a ramp at an angle, the truck can rotate in a horizontal circle. So the front stays in front and the back stays in back. But the truck still turns in a full circle. The corkscrew is hard to predict, though. So many crashes happened as a result of the corkscrew stunt that Monster Jam banned it.

WHEELIES AND DONUTS

A standard wheelie is lifting up the front tires of the truck while the back tires stay on the ground. But in a nose wheelie, the truck faces downward while its back wheels go up. While that's happening, the driver shifts from forward to reverse. It can be tricky because the drivers can't see what they're doing. They can only see dirt!

During a side wheelie, the wheels on one side of the truck stay on the ground. But the opposite side wheels lift off

FUN FACT

Bari Musawwir and Zombie hold the world record for most consecutive donuts in a monster truck. In 2020, they spun 58 times in a row.

Bicycle stunt

Donut

the ground. This stunt is sometimes called a bicycle. Driver Ryan Anderson holds the world record for longest side wheelie. He drove Son-uva Digger 891 feet, 10.8 inches (272 m) on two side wheels in 2020.

In a donut, the truck's wheels stay mostly on the ground, as the truck spins in circles. It throws out dirt from the track while it spins.

Nose wheelie

CRUSH CARS

One of the first stunts a monster truck ever did was crush a car. That was done by Bigfoot in the early 1980s. For many years, it was popular for monster trucks to drive or jump over a line of old cars at events. Sometimes, courses used a van or a car next to a van so that trucks could climb a little higher.

These crush cars come from a junkyard. Sometimes, they're free, and sometimes, event planners buy them. To make a car ready for crushing, a few things need to happen. The glass windows are taken out. Without windows, there isn't any shattered glass that could injure drivers. All of the liquids in the engine are taken out too. Many of those liquids are flammable and could catch fire. Leaking liquids also isn't good for the environment.

Black Stallion crushes cars at a county fair.

Old cars stacked up in a junkyard

Sometimes, the crush cars are filled with bales of hay. This way, the cars don't get squashed down quite so much. They can maintain their shape. As a result, the last monster truck to drive over the cars will have an experience much like the first monster truck to drive over them.

MONSTER TRUCK TRIVIA

Around 2015, Monster Jam stopped using crush cars in its events. This was at least partly because, after a crush, the flying car pieces could be dangerous. Some people say it was also becoming more difficult to find cars to crush. Crush cars are less common in monster truck events these days, but the stunt is still sometimes featured.

DRIVER SAFETY GEAR

At the beginning of the sport, monster truck drivers could wear whatever they wanted when they were behind the wheel. But over the years, a lot of safety rules have been added to the sport. Some of these include regulations about driver clothing.

These days, a driver can't just climb into the cab of a monster truck wearing everyday clothes. First, drivers wear a fire-resistant suit, which is designed to not catch on fire. These suits generally have at least three layers. Shoes must also be fire-resistant. They also have a very thin sole, or bottom, so that drivers can feel the gas and brake pedals. Fire-resistant gloves are made with a special material that helps grip the steering wheel.

Special clothing keeps drivers safe.

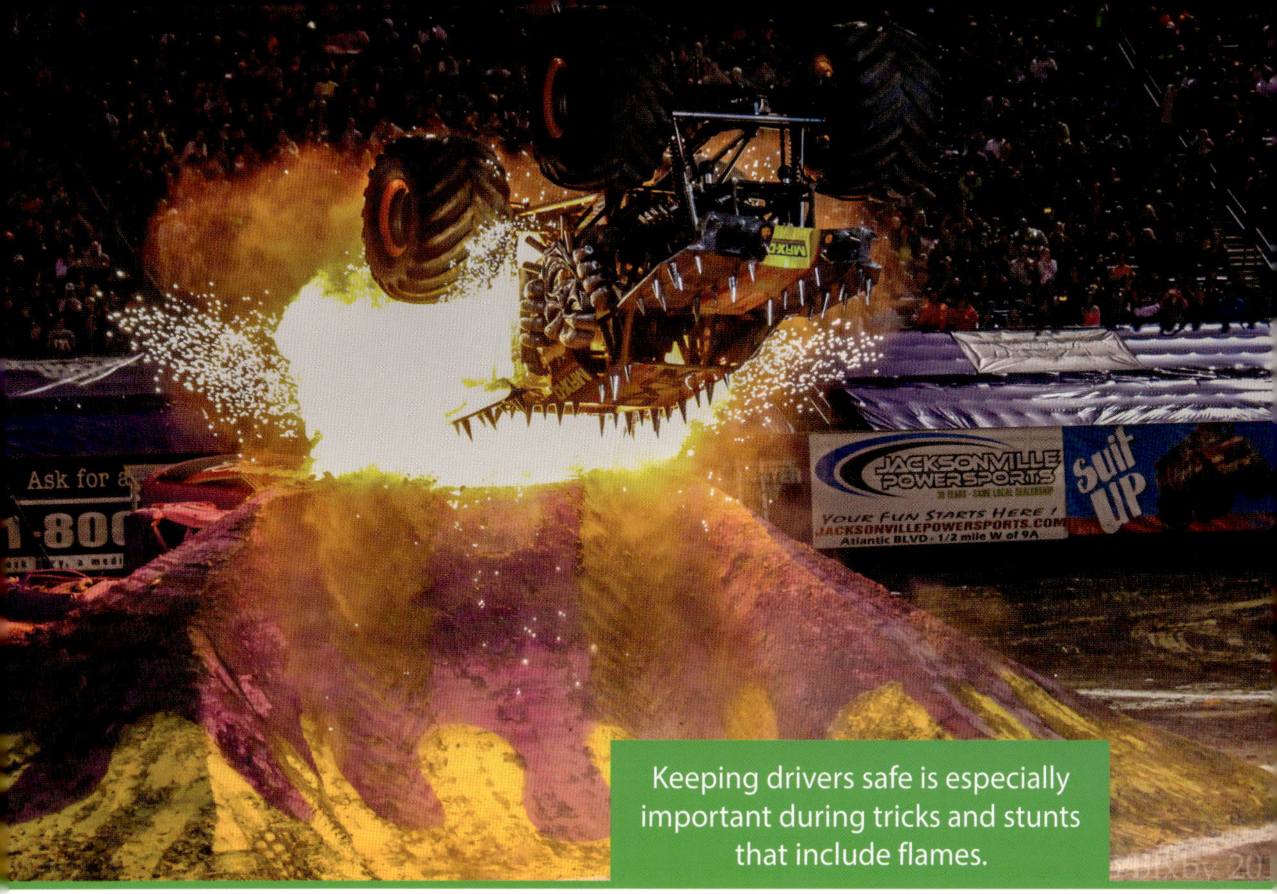

Keeping drivers safe is especially important during tricks and stunts that include flames.

Finally, drivers must wear both a fire-resistant helmet as well as eye protection. Sometimes, the eye protection is built into the helmet, but it doesn't have to be. Most drivers use helmets that attach to the truck's safety harness. That keeps the driver in place, even if the truck is flying through the air or lands upside down.

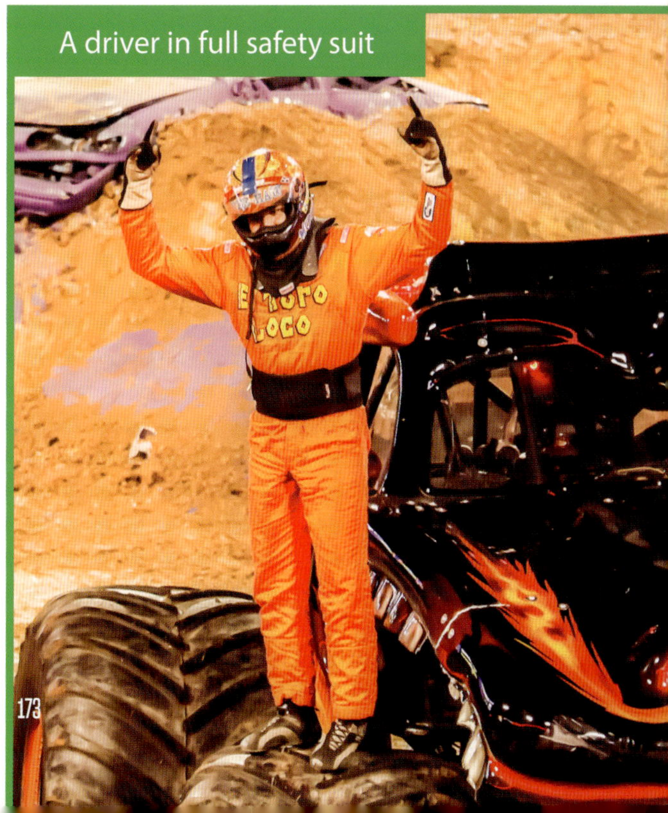

A driver in full safety suit

FANDOM

The world of monster trucks loves its fans as much as its fans love it. Drivers and crew know that without fans, there would be no monster truck events. Monster Jam and most other truck events are family friendly. A show's audience will likely include lots of kids.

As with other sports, fans often have favorite trucks or teams. They wear hats or shirts to support their trucks. Fans follow their favorites on social media and attend events where their favorite trucks will compete. Some truck teams even have their own fan clubs. Fans who sign up can get updates on the trucks, as well as discounts on fan merchandise. Some truck events have fan clubs too. Members might get to buy tickets before everyone else.

Monster Jam thinks fans are so important that they get to judge one of the events! After a truck does its freestyle run, the audience can rate the run from 1 to 10. The truck with the highest score from the audience wins the freestyle event.

A fan gets an autograph from the driver of Grave Digger.

At most monster truck events, there are opportunities, either before or after, for fans to meet drivers and see the trucks up close.

MERCHANDISE AND TOYS

Monster truck toys are almost as popular as full-sized monster trucks. Fans can buy mini versions of their favorites. Hot Wheels makes a series of monster trucks, focusing on the trucks that are part of its Monster Trucks Live show. The toys are made to scale, at 1:64. That means the actual truck is 64 times the size of the toy. Lego makes kits for people who want to build their own trucks.

Another option for racing at home is remote-controlled monster trucks. A company called Traxxas makes trucks that can go 30 miles (48 km) per hour. They're even waterproof, so they can race in the rain.

Hot Wheels toy

Monster Jam sells toys, shirts, and even bedsheets. They have plush trucks for snuggling and metal and plastic trucks for racing. The Guinness World Record for largest display of monster truck toys is held by Monster Jam and Spin Master. On October 29, 2022, they gathered 10,005 monster truck toys in Orlando, Florida. Monster Jam also has its own series of video games.

Grave Digger toy

Remote-controlled toy

A video game featuring Maximum Destruction

Monster trucks have been in many TV shows and movies, like *Ready Player One*.

POP CULTURE

In 1981, the legendary Bigfoot was the first monster truck to be in a movie. A later version of Bigfoot appeared in the 2018 sci-fi movie *Ready Player One*. In 1984, Bigfoot's rival Bearfoot appeared in a music video from the band ZZ Top. It was also in two commercials and a TV show called *Knight Rider*.

Monster trucks have made it into lots of TV shows over the years. Swamp Thing was on *ScrapHeap Challenge*. Obsession was on *House MD*. Lil' Devil was on *Men & Motors* and *The Race*. Gas Monkey Garage was featured in the British reality show *Fast N' Loud*.

Dozens of video games feature monster trucks. Monster Jam even has a whole series of its own. A few popular games include *Monster Truck Destruction*, *Monster Truck Xtreme Racing*, *Monster Jam Steel Titans*, and *Monster 4X4: Masters of Metal*.

Many monster trucks run on methanol. Even Bigfoot, the first monster truck ever, used methanol. This fuel has more power than the gas that powers automobiles. That helps monster trucks perform such amazing jumps and stunts. Methanol is also cheaper and cleaner than gas.

In recent years, a few trucks have started using diesel fuel. Diesel trucks use less fuel than methanol-powered trucks. In 2018, BroDozer competed in Monster Jam. This diesel-powered truck made it to fourth place. But not many trucks use diesel fuel.

In 2012, Bob Chandler's Bigfoot racing team released the first electric monster truck. Bigfoot 20 used six batteries for steering and brakes. Another 30 batteries powered the engine and related parts.

FUN FACT

A monster truck goes through 3 gallons (11 l) of methanol per minute.

BroDozer is one of only a few diesel-powered monster trucks.

Firestone
BIGFOOT
ODYSSE
Firestone

SPONSORSHIPS

It costs hundreds of thousands of dollars to build and maintain a monster truck. Most people or small companies can't do it without help. That's why most monster trucks have sponsors. Sponsorship means that a company or person pays the truck owner in exchange for advertising on the truck.

Bigfoot, the first monster truck, was a Ford. Ford sponsored Bigfoot for 23 years. Another big sponsor in the early years of the sport was the tire maker Firestone. It makes sense for both the truck and the sponsor if their audience and customer are the same. So a tire company might be a good sponsor since the audience knows a truck needs good tires.

Firestone not only sponsors Bigfoot, but it also supplies the truck's tires.

Sponsors pay for banners as a way to advertise at events.

Monster Jam also gets sponsorships. Some of its sponsors have included auto parts stores and tire companies. The sponsors pay to advertise their products in programs and at events. Lots of fans will see those ads.

Monster Jam has a big partnership with Marvel Comics. Together, Monster Jam can build trucks based on Marvel characters, including Iron Man and Black Panther. Hot Wheels makes toys based on the Marvel monster trucks. Monster Jam makes their own toys based on the other monster trucks that are not Marvel characters.

A Hot Wheels Spider-Man toy includes its own stunt ramp.

WORLD RECORDS

FASTEST SPEED

- Joe Sylvester in Bad Habit, August 6, 2022
- 101.8 miles per hour (164 kmh)

LONGEST RAMP JUMP

- Joe Sylvester in Bad Habit, September 1, 2013
- 237 feet, 7 inches (72 m)

HIGHEST RAMP JUMP

- Krysten Anderson in Grave Digger, June 25, 2020
- 33 feet, 9.6 inches (10 m)

LONGEST MONSTER TRUCK WHEELIE

- Adam Anderson in
  Grave Digger,
  June 25, 2020
- 624 feet, 10.4 inches (191 m)

LONGEST NOSE WHEELIE, A.K.A. STOPPIE

- Tom Meents in
  Max-D,
  June 25, 2020
- 209 feet, 2.6 inches (64 m)

MOST MONSTER TRUCKS JUMPED BY A MONSTER TRUCK

- Adam Anderson in Megalodon, June 25, 2020
- 8 monster trucks jumped

BIGGEST MONSTER TRUCK

- Bigfoot 5, 1986
- 15.5 feet (5 m) tall, 38,000 pounds (17,237 kg)

LONGEST MONSTER TRUCK

- Sin City Hustler
- Jen and Brad Campbell of Big Toyz Racing
- 32 feet (10 m) long

LONGEST MONSTER TRUCK JUMP IN REVERSE

- Michael Vaters in Black Stallion, 2002
- 70 feet (21 m)

FIRST MONSTER TRUCK TO JUMP OVER A BOEING 747

- Dan Runte in Bigfoot 14, 1999
- Distance jumped: 202 feet (62 m)

GLOSSARY

chassis
The frame of a vehicle.

encore
A small, extra performance after an event.

fabrication
Constructing or manufacturing.

fiberglass
A strong insulating material made from very fine glass fibers. It is used to make things such as buildings, cars, and boats.

fire-resistant
Able to be near fire or extreme heat without catching fire or allowing heat to go through it to the non-heated side.

horsepower
A unit to measure the power of an engine.

merch
Short for "merchandise," which are goods for purchase, often showing logos or artwork from a specific person or group.

methanol
A type of wood alcohol that is mostly used for making fuels and substances that make other substances dissolve. It is colorless, flammable, and poisonous to humans.

modifying
Making changes to something.

off-road
Driving a vehicle in a place with no streets or designated paths.

rival
Someone or something that one is trying to beat in competition.

rookie
An athlete in their first season of a professional sport.

sponsor
To pay the costs of a truck or event in exchange for having one's products advertised.

supercharge
To add charge to an engine's intake at a pressure higher than the air around it.

suspension
The part of a car that has springs to make the car stable, protecting it from the road and helping the driver keep control of the vehicle.

tractor pull
A motorsport in which specialized tractors drag a metal sled that increases in weight as it goes. The tractor that pulls the sled the farthest is the winner.

welding
Heating metal objects or materials and then sticking them together.

FURTHER READING

Abdo, Kenny. *Monster Truck Rallies*. ABDO, 2019.

Abdo, Kenny. *Monster Trucks*. ABDO, 2024.

Gifford, Clive. *Monster Trucks*. Firefly Books, 2019.

Rogers, Marie. *Monster Trucks*. PowerKids Press, 2021.

ONLINE RESOURCES

To learn more about monster trucks, please visit **abdobooklinks.com** or scan this QR code. These links are routinely monitored and updated to provide the most current information available.

INDEX

ABDOBOOKS.COM

Published by Abdo Reference, a division of ABDO, PO Box 398166, Minneapolis, Minnesota 55439. Copyright © 2025 by Abdo Consulting Group, Inc. International copyrights reserved in all countries. No part of this book may be reproduced in any form without written permission from the publisher. Encyclopedias™ is a trademark and logo of Abdo Reference.

Printed in China
092024
012025

Editor: Carrie Hasler
Series Designer: Colleen McLaren

LIBRARY OF CONGRESS CONTROL NUMBER: 2023949483

PUBLISHER'S CATALOGING-IN-PUBLICATION DATA
Names: Kuehl, Ashley, author.
Title: The monster trucks encyclopedia / by Ashley Kuehl
Description: Minneapolis, Minnesota : Abdo Reference, 2025 | Series: Motorsports encyclopedias | Includes online resources and index.
Identifiers: ISBN 9781098294427 (lib. bdg.) | ISBN 9798384913696 (ebook)
Subjects: LCSH: Motorsports--Juvenile literature. | Motor racing--Juvenile literature. | Automobile racing--Juvenile literature. | Monster trucks--Juvenile literature. | Races (Sports)--Juvenile literature. | Encyclopedias and dictionaries--Juvenile literature.
Classification: DDC 796.72--dc23